STAR PALMS

Sue Armstrong

London
VICTOR GOLLANCZ LTD
1988

First published in Great Britain 1988
by Victor Gollancz Ltd,
14 Henrietta Street, London WC2E 8QJ

A Gollancz Paperback Original

© Sue Armstrong 1988

British Library Cataloguing in Publication Data
Armstrong, Sue
   Star palms.
   1. Palmistry — Personal
   observations
   I. Title
   133.6′092′4

   ISBN 0-575-04366-0

1981-1988

**Mountains, friends, family and loved ones
Animals past and present.
...My Guide...**

This book is sold subject to the condition that it
shall not, by way of trade or otherwise, be lent,
resold, hired out, or otherwise circulated
without the publisher's prior consent in any
form of binding or cover other than that in
which it is published and without a similar
condition including this condition being
imposed on the subsequent purchaser.

Photoset in Great Britain by
Rowland Phototypesetting Ltd,
Bury St Edmunds and London

Printed in Italy by New Interlitho

CONTENTS

FOREWORD

I have thoroughly enjoyed the writing of this book and all the unusual adventures my research took me on. I'd like to express my heartfelt thanks to all the brave participants, who have willingly allowed me to ink their palms and speak openly about their characters. My curiosity prompted me to look for an outstanding common denominator between these talented people, but I was surprised by the outcome; it wasn't at all what I expected. Instead of a wealth of markings indicating charmed lives I found the most energetic influence was in fact Jupiter and Mars, the sign of drive and persistence. All these personalities have the ability to overcome any difficult phase; they have endless bounce, enthusiasm and dedication. It was amazing to find such strength in so many people. It seems to me, therefore, that it's their gifts of courage and perseverance more than mere luck which has contributed to their success. Moreover, the majority of the palms studied here bear out my belief that we all have a guiding spirit, which, if heeded, will support and encourage us throughout our lives.

SUE ARMSTRONG

'Sceptical, I'd said "yes" to Sue Armstrong with some curiosity, mostly to be nice. Then came shivers of recognition and some alarm at being so uncannily uncovered. "There isn't anyone else this could be except you," said a close friend.'
SUSANNAH YORK

'When Sue Armstrong came to the studios to read my palms I was immediately aware of her warmth and insight. At that time I was not the happiest person in the world and Sue "knew" of this in her analysis. I thank her for her guidance and advice.'
BILL TREACHER

'I have to say that Sue Armstrong's analysis of my palm is frighteningly accurate – for better or worse! Still, if it's good enough for President Reagan, I guess a little "outside help" is good enough for me!'
FRED DINENAGE

PALM READING
A Beginner's Guide

The study of palms is endlessly intriguing. With it you can discover the opportunities that lie within you and get to know yourself and others better. Because this book leans towards the light-hearted rather than the more serious aspects of the art, these basic guidelines for interpreting palms are kept to a minimum. The enthusiast can read up further on the scientific background and with a little patience can soon become an ardent student of palmistry.

Always remember that a right-handed individual should be read from left to right and vice versa for a left-handed person. The left hand (of a right-handed person) normally contains the secret of life, the genetic and hereditary structure of the innermost nature: the basic map of your life. The right reveals the progressive elements and is known as the current hand, telling of past and present events and revealing future possibilities. It also shows if the personality has altered in any way (major or insignificant) or if opportunities shown in the left hand have been rejected. We can follow through from the plan of life on the left palm to the right, uncovering the various patterns. For a left-handed person you would read from right to left, thus the left hand is the active hand.

What is also important to remember is that while an expert reading of a palm can reveal the hidden depths of a personality and possible past and future influences, the termination of life is very rarely in evidence. You can see cessation periods and perhaps life-threatening conditions, but in my experience losses in the hand usually refer to someone close to my client. Finally you must bear in mind that the palms can alter with time and the hand print studied today may not be the same tomorrow.

There are four main areas to study.
1. *Skin Texture*
2. *Flexibility*
3. *Shape, size and length of palm and fingers*
4. *Lines, markings and symbols*

1. SKIN TEXTURE
Generally, very soft flabby skin indicates a sensitive and gullible individual. The firmer your skin the better sense of inner control you'll have. Overly soft and fragile skin would make you extremely vulnerable to atmosphere and environment. If the skin is tough then the opposite applies, making for someone lacking feeling, with a thick outer shell for protection against the ups and downs of life.

2. FLEXIBILITY
When someone's hand is easy to manipulate and bends back and forth without any sign of resistance then they're usually easy-going, generous and quite impressionable. If the opposite applies then you would find them set in routine. Indeed, they can be too fixed in their ways and refuse to accept other points of view.

3. SHAPE, SIZE AND LENGTH OF PALM AND FINGERS
First impressions very often come from the overall shape of the hand. Is the palm narrow in one area and wider in another? Do the fingers lean away from, or do they rely on, each other? Do they look extra long (or too short) for the overall hand appearance? All these things must be assessed before any definite interpretation can be confirmed. Therefore, it is important to look first at the palm itself. Is it long, square, round, oval, large or small? Are the fingers fat, thin, short or long, or even misshapen (eliminating of course any physical abnormality)? For example, if we look at a fat, dumpy little palm – round with short fingers – then we see an individual with outgoing energies, lots of physical enthusiasm, one with bounce and artistic leanings. But longish fingers and palms reveal the owner to be dreamy, slow, less impulsive, more thoughtful and analytical, and certainly fairly creative. They may, of course, be full of schemes and visions which they are unable to put into action.

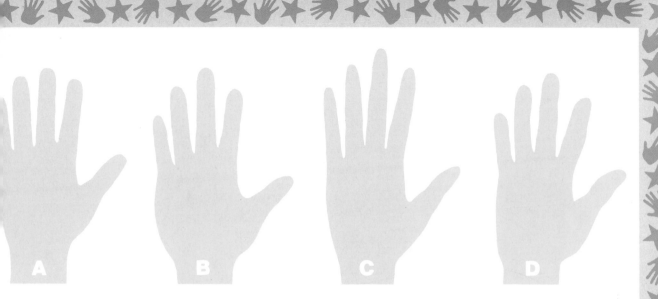

Square *(Shape A)* Square hands, like Cynthia Payne's, exude great strength, reliability and firmness. The structure appears solid and enthusiastic offering a safe approach to life. People with square hands (noted, by the way, more on men than women) usually show themselves as builders, lawyers or business people. The square-handed character prefers routine and respects law and order. These hands usually have short fingers and square tips.

Round *(Shape B)* Roy Kinnear's are a good example of round hands. They have a circular appearance full of flesh and bursting with life, adventure and challenge. Rounded palms are often red and look 'fit to burst'. Their owners tend to be fiery spirits, enjoying arty and cultural pleasures. They adore travel and would have a far better ability to adapt to change than the square-handed person – but their impulsiveness may give them problems!

Artistic *(Shape C)* The artistic hand is smooth and longish, denoting a finely-tuned individual. The fingertips are pointed or rounded and everything about the hand appears long and stretchy. We have here someone who adores beauty in music, the arts and so on – with a delicate disposition that is sensitive to life and to people, and very often psychic. Both Nick Lyndhurst's and Sue Cook's left hands are artistic.

Mixed *(Shape D)* The mixed hand can be a contradictory one to describe and indeed, to analyse. It houses the ingredients of all the shapes and looks slightly spatulate, combining a confusing mixture of physical elements: wide and narrow, long and short. The owner like Susannah York will have quite a versatile and enthusiastic nature; realistic yet sensitive, inquisitive and full of energy.

Thumbs Palmists in the East tend to take the thumbs as the rulers of the palms, focusing most of their reading on them. The Western palmist tends to generalise more on the make-up of the whole hand, but never forgets the importance of this isolated joint. You will find that the thumb is as flexible as the palm and fingers; sometimes more so. A very flexible thumb with a strong outward turn at the tip denotes someone who is vulnerable and generous. The firmer the thumb and the more it is held inward the more rigid the nature is. The positioning is also important. A very low-set thumb shows a free and easy, uninhibited attitude that would be suffocated by too much restriction. A high-set thumb (one set nearer to the forefinger) indicates a tendency towards self-indulgence. The person would have high, perhaps old-fashioned morals, and would tend to be narrow-minded.

The shaping of the thumb tends to have some say here too. A clubbed type (thick and bulbous at the tip) reveals someone to be extremely sharp and quick-tempered – this kind of thumb is also aptly known as Murderers' Thumb! The waisted thumb (waisting inward at the lower phalange) reveals a person with little self control and a weak will. Such people are very friendly characters but can be swayed too much by others and therefore tend to be a little vulnerable. A plump large thumb indicates a highly nervous disposition, slightly erratic and difficult to get along with.

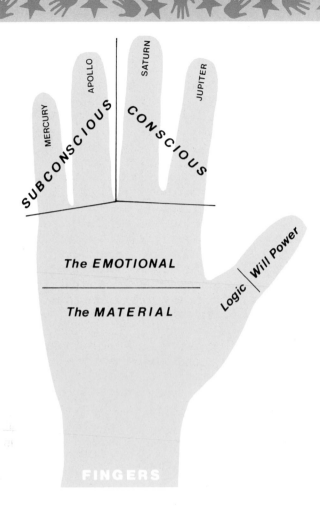

FINGERS

SUBCONSCIOUS

CONSCIOUS

MERCURY

APOLLO

SATURN

JUPITER

The EMOTIONAL

The MATERIAL

Logic | Will Power

The MOUNTS

1st Phalange
Mental & Spiritual

2nd Phalange
Practical

3rd Phalange
Physical

APOLLO   SATURN JUPITER

MERCURY

UPPER MARS

LOWER MARS

NEPTUNE

MOON

VENUS

Fingers How do your fingers look when you lay your hand out before you? Do they nestle closely together or stand apart? Is one very much longer than the others? Extra length in any one finger implies a dominance of its energy. The **Saturn** finger is generally the longest; it rules the palm and contains the energies of both the subconscious and the conscious. A straight, upright Saturn finger displays a balance between emotion (the subconscious) and will (the conscious). It is the finger of solitude and inner strength, independence and self-confidence.

The **Apollo** finger represents your love of beauty, the arts and people; the **Jupiter** finger your assertiveness, ambitions and ideals. Their tips should reach just below the tip of Saturn for a happy balance between the three. The **Mercury** – finger of communication – tip should just touch the top of the second phalange of the Apollo finger.

Wide and airy spacing of the fingers suggests an outgoing and confident personality, but since the fingers relate to *desires* more than to *will* this confidence only comes by exercising your will. If the fingers lie closely together this shows you need company and support from other people.

The **Phalanges** are equally important and you must look to see how large they are in relation to the rest of the hand: the thicker and/or longer the phalange the more dominant the qualities it denotes. The phalanges are divided into three sections. The top phalange represents emotions, thoughts and spirituality – mental interpretation of things. The middle shows us the practical level – how we react with our logic and reason, how we cope with the material aspects of life. The third and lowest is interpreted from a physical angle – how active we can be, how much we appreciate the enjoyments and luxuries in life.

You must also remember to study the **mounts**: Venus, Mercury, Apollo, Saturn, Jupiter, Moon, Upper Mars and Lower Mars. What these areas of the hand denote is outlined in the Astrological notes under 'Ruling Planets'. When analysing a mount, look to see how significant it is: is it raised extra high in the hand? If so, then that particular energy is emphasised. If the mount is lifeless and flat then the energy which is produced is at a reduced level.

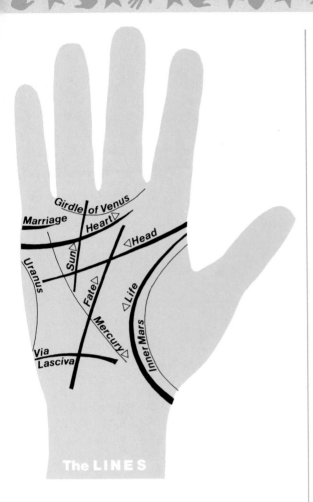

Girdle of Venus
Marriage
Heart◁
◁Head
Uranus
Sun◁
Fate◁
◁Life
Mercury◁
Inner Mars
Via Lasciva

The LINES

LINES, MARKINGS AND SYMBOLS

The lines on the hand help us to understand a lot more about the character and about possible changes to come. I always take the halfway point on the line to mean mid-life and judge age accordingly. Although it is impossible to shrink into this mini-synopsis a serious study of all the various line shapings, here are just a few hints:

Clear and undisturbed lines depict complete balance, but these are seldom found.

Lines ending with a fork usually reveal good balance within that energy.

Extra long lines portray more of that particular energy level; shorter than usual, and the opposite often applies.

A red and aggressive-looking line shows frustration, anger and tension. A fine, over-delicate marking reveals timidity.

Heart Line The heart line indicates the depth and quality of your feelings. For instance, a very curved and deeply-cut line shows you have deep feelings and generosity. The heart line commences where

the marriage area is outlined and you read up it towards the Jupiter or Saturn finger. A line ending under Jupiter is about the most evenly balanced. If it extends too far – beyond Jupiter – it can indicate driving passions and obsessions. On the other hand, if it shirks its responsibilities, ending below Saturn or even shorter, it suggests a much cooler, sharper and perhaps more self-indulgent personality. The heart line can also indicate the strength of the physical organ. If thin and cold-looking the heart is not functioning correctly, especially if the line looks slightly blue.

Girdle of Venus This reflects romantic and sensual aspects of the personality, emphasising sexual behaviour. If it's present in your palm it shows you are a warm, charismatic personality. And if it's broken and scattered it indicates an even greater sensitivity towards the sexual side of life!

Head Line The line commences between thumb and Jupiter finger (i.e. at birth) and is read across the palm, it offers us an insight into the mentality, brain power and thinking process. When the line is clear and unbroken and runs straight across the palm the character thinks logically and is never mentally cluttered. Variations in the line – if it is misshapen, broken or frayed-looking – enable us to gauge the difference in the mental energies from one person to another. A very short head line for instance, maybe ending under the Apollo finger, would give a very impulsive and quick-thinking mentality, yet the longer the head line the more one is prone to worrying and analysing issues at length. A head line ending under the Mercury mount is roughly average. This reveals fair intelligence and normal powers of analysis, providing it does not slope too heavily into the Moon mount, which shows moody tendencies and a fertile imagination! If the heart and head line are close together this will often show a somewhat narrow-minded character, but the more spacious the gap, the more open-minded the individual.

The experienced palmist can also detect hearing or eye problems through analysis of the line, as well as mental disorders.

Life Line This is the barometer of your life force and with it you can study your progress through life. Breaks in the line indicate general disturbances: major changes such as home moves, career changes, travel, emigration, marriage. These are often for our own good, giving us breathing space to re-evaluate our lives. But this line is also known as the stomach line and can reveal internal disorders or major operations. Obviously one wants to see a nice clear line without any breaks or interruptions; these, however, are rare. Again, the length of the line is important. Forget the old wives' tale about a longer line meaning a longer life; I have not found this to be true. The longer the line the more energy and vital force we are able to store, and therefore, the better we are able to carry out demanding tasks. A shorter line will often disturb that internal balance. The energy force would be weakened and at some stage, mainly where the line ends, we would have to reassess our progress. It may mean that a vastly different way of living must be accepted at the age when the line terminates, especially if the fate line takes over and drives on strongly up the hand. Any circles or loops along the life line indicate periods of difficulty, or isolated incidents which can be very taxing and draining. If the life line suddenly breaks but re-joins a little later, then this normally refers to a major re-adjustment in lifestyle, either through major illness or a dramatic change in conditions.

As with the head line the life line stems from the birth area between the thumb and Jupiter finger and is read down the palm. It should be fairly rounded, gracing the outskirts of mount Venus. If too tightly embracing the thumb it suggests a person who can be cool and unresponsive, secretive or introverted; if wide and expanding across the hand then we see an outward-motivated, giving character.

Fate Line This can stem from anywhere on the palm and is read upwards, no matter where it starts. Again, it is best unbroken for it determines our spiritual progress, our faith and inner constitution. Breaks accurately reflect the major events that *must* take place in our lives to move us on and redirect us – moves that we have perhaps been too lazy to initiate ourselves until Destiny intervenes. You should consider where it starts and also its direction: the mounts it travels to and the lines it links with indicate directions a life may take. I believe the interpretation of the fate line is one of the palmist's most valuable skills and that you should always follow its promptings.

Via Lasciva Once this line denoted a drug user, or a lustful, social vulture. It represented all the forbidden, tempting aspects of life. These days we view it with much less vindictiveness. It emphasises enjoyment of all kinds, a robust nature, sensual and full of flavour – someone who revels in good food and wine and fun-loving exploits.

Mercury Line I find the Mercury line (sometimes called the Health/Liver line) the most uncomfortable one to come to terms with, because throughout my studies I have discovered so many meanings to it. Basically, if unbroken and wavy, it indicates a delicate constitution. A more straightforward-looking line shows someone with fewer physical worries. Not everyone possesses it and its presence tends to indicate a highly-strung disposition.

Uranus Line This curious and fascinating little marking reveals our intuitive responses. People with these markings seem to pick things up instantly and have a telepathic rapport with others. Their spiritual communication is usually very active, although some are fearful of this sixth sense and sadly, because of lack of understanding, they fail to use this extra faculty – which after all is a natural, inbuilt skill given to us for a purpose!

Sun/Apollo Line Usually running up the hand towards the Apollo mount, this represents success whether it be personal or material. It gives us wealth and assures achievements. It's a lucky line and if unbroken and fairly long suggests tremendous recognition in life.

Marriage/Relationship Lines These horizontal lines are usually seen on the outer area of the palm above the heart line and they suggest opportunities in love. The longer the lines the more likely it is that a relationship will remain devoted and stable. Breaks or splits on the line suggest separation or distance between the partners; lines that slope down towards the heart line show disappointment in love. Children may be identified by the vertical lines stemming from the marriage lines; longer lines implying male children, shorter ones implying female. An abundance of lines suggests that you are very fertile. Other relationships, both friendships and more serious liaisons, are noted by the vertical lines on mount Venus.

A multitude of lines covering the hands There are two aspects to be taken into account here. Firstly, the usual interpretation of such intense line activity relates to a very highly-strung, active person, ruled by his mind and living off a high level of nervous energy. Secondly, I see this as a sign of learning: the individual would have a great capacity for absorbing knowledge, mostly in the spiritual sense. This can often indicate someone who has lived through several incarnations on Earth.

SYMBOLS

It is extremely difficult to cram into a few pages all the meanings of the various symbols one may find on palms, but here is a brief and generalised guide.

Star A fortunate sign. It usually encourages prosperity and material well-being. Look upon it always as a mark of approval – a very good sign to be blessed with.

cle The circle symbolises just that, the fact that
often run around in circles getting nowhere fast!
k at the circle as a time when things have to take
r time. Maybe fate is asking you to be patient?
s sign could be seen as a blockage.

p or Island Another off-putting sign, implying
need for thought and often bringing with it
fusion and worry. It is therefore not really a
lthy-looking symbol, mainly because it puts up
riers and slows us down.

uare This may imply danger of some sort, but
offers protection from that danger.
ventative measures should be taken when these
rnings are visible in the hand.

angle The triangle symbolises material gain – a
eficial and encouraging symbol.

ss Sadly, this is an unfavourable sign, indicating
ss of some sort – of a loved one or a possession.
t remember that unkind markings are often
ssings in disguise since they prepare us for the
ning danger.

ille Usually found on the mounts, this suggests
air of frustration: disputes if located on mount
rcury, emotional or domestic conflict if on
nus.

stique Cross This outstanding sign reveals a
at sensitivity and creative intuition. It allows the
dividual to rely on his instincts and inner feelings,
owing off an air of sound judgement. It will often
pear on the hands of the occultist or religious
thusiast and is a symbol of mystical abilities. It is
ays located between the head and the heart line.

AN INSIGHT INTO MY WAY OF INTERPRETATION

Anyone can learn the basic scientific study of palmistry, but without the inner inspiration, psychic ability, spiritual guide – call it what you will – the student cannot paint a complete picture. When I begin to interpret someone's palms I put aside immediately their birth sign, so I'm not swayed against my inner feelings, although it is interesting to refer to it *after* analysis to see where the palm bears out the implications of the sign and where it differs. I carry out the steps I've outlined and then I allow the combination of study and intuition to take over. Others may prefer to work purely from their knowledge of palmistry teachings, but my readings are infused with my spiritual response to the person in question. This way I can complete the portrait in colour rather than leaving it quietly bland in black and white.

As for reading past, present and future, well of course it is possible to highlight certain features which lurk in the various symbols and signs, but naturally one does not want to intervene where spiritual direction should be followed. It is therefore always important to help the individual to discover their own potential and if possible, outline any future opportunities, without imposing restrictions of any sort. Conditions change with the passing of years and both the lines and the hand structure are prone to change too. What is read today for instance is not necessarily going to be in the hand in the future. We often change our own destiny, or remain *in situ* when in fact we should be moving on. It helps to think of palmistry as a stepping stone, helping people with their problems, guiding them where you can, and often giving them an unusually fresh insight into their characters. Often, hidden talents are exposed, giving the owner more confidence to pursue private dreams.

Do always remember when interpreting palms that the good weighs up with the bad. No hand may be said to be wholly unreasonable – one is always seeking the positive as well as trying to divert the negative. Life is full of varying tasks and it is often up to us to accept and learn from testing periods. We cannot always change things but we can do a lot to help ourselves by learning and accepting and remaining optimistic.

A palm reader must be a sensitive, sincere and kindly creature, delicately placed towards the human race. My motto is: it is always better to give than to receive, and I like to feel that each individual whose palm I read receives as much satisfaction as I can give. It is fun learning about people's characters through such an art and I very much enjoyed meeting everyone who took part in this book. I hope that the reader will be inspired by it!

SUE ARMSTRONG

A NOTE ON ASTROLOGY

RULING PLANETS

The influence of the ruling planets is reflected in the mounts, fingers and in other areas of the hand.

Venus Rules partnerships, love, beauty and harmony. Indicates a friendly personality with a love of the arts, clothes and fashion – and possessions of all kinds.

Mercury Rules the intellect, mental perception, communications and business acumen. Those ruled by Mercury are analytical, imaginative, keen to acquire knowledge and serve the community.

Apollo The sun-influenced character is warm-hearted, kind, affectionate, creative, with a love of the theatre and good organising and designing skills. Apollo also rules the ego.

Saturn Saturn encourages the practical, constructive, self-disciplined and independent character. Cautious and selfish at times, but tolerant.

Jupiter Jupiter represents knowledge, a highly-developed mentality, confidence, self-promotion and self-esteem.

Moon Rules creativity and fertility. Moon-influenced characters are passive yet imaginative; restless and moody – and often have a good memory!

Mars Indicates anger and aggression within the individual, who will be decisive, freedom-loving and strongly sexed.

There are no mounts reflecting the last three planets but it is interesting to note what their influences in the hand represent. **Uranus** is a planet that moves the character forward through major changes in life, and denotes unpredictability. **Neptune** rules poetry, dance and music; those governed by Neptune are imaginative, idealistic, artistically creative and spiritual – often with their heads in the clouds. And finally **Pluto**, which governs new cycles and stimulation, beginnings and ends of phases in life. Those ruled by Pluto adapt well to unfortunate circumstances for they are gamblers by nature.

ELEMENTS

The characteristics of the element under which you are born can strongly influence your personality.

Fire emphasises enthusiasm, desire, spirit, creativity and anger.
Air governs communications and action.
Earth affects the reasoning senses, the practical and logical aspects of character as well as our physical and material well-being.
Water rules the emotions and our feelings and responses to others.

SUN SIGNS

Here is a table showing which elements and planets rule the twelve sun signs.

FIRE	Aries	(22 Mar – 20 Apr)	MARS
	Leo	(24 Jul – 23 Aug)	SUN (APOLLO)
	Sagittarius	(23 Nov – 22 Dec)	JUPITER
AIR	Aquarius	(20 Jan – 19 Feb)	SATURN/URANUS
	Gemini	(22 May – 22 Jun)	MERCURY
	Libra	(24 Sep – 23 Oct)	VENUS
EARTH	Taurus	(21 Apr – 21 May)	VENUS
	Virgo	(24 Aug – 23 Sep)	MERCURY
	Capricorn	(23 Dec – 19 Jan)	SATURN
WATER	Pisces	(20 Feb – 21 Mar)	NEPTUNE
	Cancer	(23 Jun – 23 Jul)	MOON
	Scorpio	(24 Oct – 22 Nov)	MARS/PLUTO

A Note on the Layout of the Hands in this book

The hands are laid out in no particular order. When only one hand print is reproduced full size it is simply because that hand is more interesting to study than the other. Therefore a right-handed person may not necessarily have their right hand pictured if the left hand is more revealing – and the same is true of left-handed stars. In every case where two palms are reproduced the past (or birth) hand is so named, to distinguish it from the current (active) hand.

STEPHANIE BEACHAM

·P·R·O·F·I·L·E·

Actress, star of *The Colbys* and *Connie*

Date of Birth: 28 February

Sun Sign: PISCES

Element: Water

Ruling Planet: Neptune

S how biz and theatrical hands tend to be very sensitive, so I was surprised to find that the skin on Stephanie's palms had a rather stiff texture. Yet oddly enough there was no sign of stiffness when I manipulated her hand. This is a formidable combination, giving the owner strength and superiority and the confidence to handle the stresses and strains of life.

A STRONG SHELL

Both her Jupiter fingers leant away backwards from the hand in a very marked manner, which implies a dominance of the Jupiter energies – forceful, driving fingers making for a forceful, commanding woman with boundless initiative. No time for ditherers; no tolerating fools gladly; no hesitation in speaking her mind; in fact, her feathers are probably too easily ruffled! Her strong will and brisk nature are reflected in the thick base of the thumb and I detected large reserves of inner strength to face and withstand any trauma.

Stephanie's hands show aggression, passion, desire and an active, powerful personality.

The Mars mounts are fleshy and dominant giving her plenty of 'attack'. These planetary influences highlight her stamina but her ruling planet Neptune would not allow the sensitive and curious side to be hidden for too long.

... WITH A SOFT CENTRE

Where Stephanie reveals the other side of her nature – the sensitive side – is in her possessive, clinging heart line. It shows her to be deeply aware of others' opinions, wounded by harsh words and quick to respond to criticism. There is a

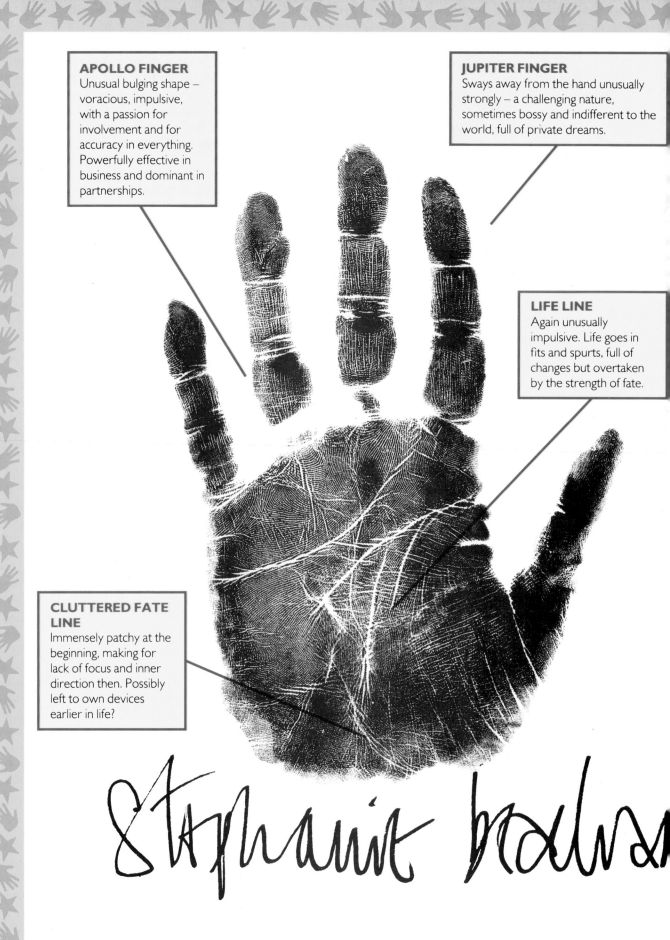

APOLLO FINGER
Unusual bulging shape –
voracious, impulsive,
with a passion for
involvement and for
accuracy in everything.
Powerfully effective in
business and dominant in
partnerships.

JUPITER FINGER
Sways away from the hand unusually
strongly – a challenging nature,
sometimes bossy and indifferent to the
world, full of private dreams.

LIFE LINE
Again unusually
impulsive. Life goes in
fits and spurts, full of
changes but overtaken
by the strength of fate.

**CLUTTERED FATE
LINE**
Immensely patchy at the
beginning, making for
lack of focus and inner
direction then. Possibly
left to own devices
earlier in life?

THE PAST HAND

softer person within the cool, sharp exterior who can respond to life with remarkable warmth once she stops hiding behind her outer armour. This gentle, passionate side to her could well be overlooked on first meeting.

You can see how long her heart line is, and how with the powerfully wide mount of Venus it dominates the hand. This could well lead to problems in dealing with people if her overpowering energy isn't kept in check, for her drive and spirit is such that she may be blind to her rejection of others. Yet if she is hard on others she is no less hard on herself: that fiery spirit will push her to the limit to achieve her desires and ambitions. The impulsive head line and the influence of Jupiter can make her imprudent as she tends to act on instinct, but this is counterbalanced by the clearly outlined knuckles indicating someone who reflects on life. Stephanie still needs to take time out sometimes to ponder the direction her life is taking and regain personal balance.

QUICKSILVER PSYCHE

While Stephanie is basically earthbound the fate and head lines cross in the centre palm and there are further crosses between the head and heart lines, which suggest psychic awareness and an active subconscious. There are acute lines running through the Neptune area, showing that imagination and fantasies sometimes overtake reality. The head line pumps out short, sharp energies; together with the upright thumbs this suggests a quicksilver mentality and outspoken nature. There's no doubt this aggressiveness gives Stephanie's health a real boost, and although the forces in the palm come in fits and starts they're very commanding when active: a constant smouldering fire that surges rapidly into flame!

A CRY IN THE WILDERNESS?

It must be said that there are sad signs in these palms, making me feel that there've been crises in the past when Stephanie's inner self was confused – tormented even – and she was left wondering who and where she was. The head line on the left (past) hand is disturbed by the many single lines that cross it at random showing vulnerability and some indecisiveness in the mental sphere. But in the current hand the head line does become stronger and clearer which means Stephanie is on more secure ground these days; life is opening up for her, giving her free rein to exercise her lively, up-and-at-'em spirit. It's possible that something in her childhood may have introduced the need to fight or retaliate in some way, and this may well be the reason she strives so hard today. She's certainly a fighter and you can't but admire her endurance.

As I've said, Stephanie is undoubtedly a down-to-earth person – you can see the size of the palms outweighs the fingers, showing how she delights in material pleasures. Yet, although the palms are basically square in shape, her artistic nature is reflected in the lively talent lines above the heart line. She needs to have her efforts recognised; she's not afraid to fight for her rights – frivolous lines crossing Venus show such conflicts in the past. Although she can be demanding and dictatorial you have to applaud her sheer guts and determination. And whenever life gets on top of her you only have to look at her strong fate line to see that Destiny is waiting to step in with exciting new possibilities!

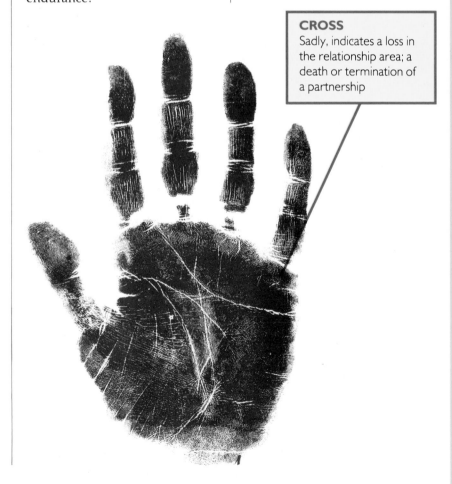

CROSS
Sadly, indicates a loss in the relationship area; a death or termination of a partnership

BARRY HUMPHRIES

·P·R·O·F·I·L·E·

Comedian, Cultural Attaché,
Dame of the British Empire

Date of Birth: 17 February 1934

Sun Sign: AQUARIUS

Element: Air

Ruling Planet: Uranus

Sudden variation of thoughts, intensity of desires, yet a friendly socialiser: three facets rule this fascinating but seriously deep man. Barry's firm skin, broad nails and moderately flexible palms support and stabilise his somewhat unpredictable, luminous nature. The long thumbs display immense intellect – the power to study at length whether it be books or merely learning from observation of the human race. These palms are bursting with unbelievable durability and variety.

A UNIQUE PERSONALITY

At one glance there is a noticeable difference in the shapes of Barry's two palms: the right artistically rounded while the left is inherently square. This squareness offers reliability; it accepts a certain amount of routine and is content with a placid, orderly lifestyle. Square-handed folk are servers of the community, so from birth Barry must have felt the need to succour others. His inbuilt desire to project himself out to the world underlies everything he does. Confidence to do so, however, comes from the encouraging talent emphasised by his rounded right palm. It

may therefore have taken him a while to realise and accept his true creative potential. Neptune, centre hand, is undisturbed by the hive of line activity dancing back and forth across Venus and Moon – unveiling an unassuming, rather bashful, deeply restrained individual. The low-set, Mars-orientated head line shows how well Barry can use his imagination, but it's not so long as to imply that he's fanciful. The lighthearted, frivolous nature is found in the rather effeminate fingers. Being fine and dainty they set a remarkably unusual contrast to such heavy, broad, masculine palms. This marked difference suggests the two aspects of his personality reflected in his stage acts.

AN AUSTRALIAN DIPLOMAT…

The raging drive in the physical, outgoing, lower right palm mirrors the active side of Barry. It is heavy and aggressive to the point of clumsiness, bordering on the brutish . . . Les Patterson?! Here lies an elementary crudeness striving to be expelled. If he couldn't find a means to express this aspect of his character he would end up a very frustrated man. Here is someone constantly involved; a doer, an entrepreneur. The amazing breadth and strength of this lower palm means that the material sphere and its rewards matter greatly to him. The level of practical intelligence can be gauged here (as well as in the head line, Mercury and fingertips). It is significant that it is enormous!

ENTER DAME EDNA!

Such willowy, abstract fingers contrast unusually with the broad palms. The fingers relate to our desires and Barry's are a major influence over and above his huge lower palms. The right hand is tantalising and artistic, especially soft and dreamy

FINGERS
Adequate space between all fingers showing freedom of thought and action. Odd shapings here and there show need for less restriction and some passing off of responsibility. He's a glutton for hard work though: the top of the palm drops dramatically down to Mercury mount, showing persistence and endurance. Note how slender and feminine the fingers are in contrast to the palms.

PALM
Much more rounded and outgoing than left. Both, however, are immoderately broad and earthy. This palm may take his actions beyond the bounds of convention. But the left shows he has a rational outlook on life. There's tremendous breadth of vision in his hands.

HEART LINE
Dipping towards the head, this shows a need for putting the practical before the emotional sometimes – but generally well balanced.

BASE OF THUMB
Three ringed markings here suggest three varying lifestyles or perhaps his three personalities – Dame Edna, Les Patterson . . . and Barry Humphries somewhere in the middle.

JUPITER FINGER
A little lack of confidence in the marked curve to Jupiter as it defers to the dominatingly long Saturn finger.

PHALANGES
Thin and long, reflecting Barry's ability to analyse and his capable streak that can make him take on too much and cause him anxiety. The length of the middle phalanges reveals his sudden seriousness and firm grasp of the commercial, the worldly and the material. The length itself shows how all these aspects are exaggerated in him.

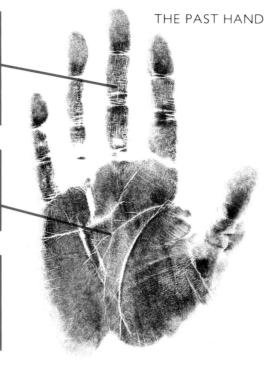

SATURN FINGER
This disillusioned area (cross) on the practical phalange reveals a major material or private loss of some kind recently.

HEAD LINE
Split reflects desire to present different aspects of his personality.

PALM
Square birth hand is reliable, placid, orderly; accepts routine and is keen to serve others.

looking, full of feminine overtones. While Mercury leans away from the other fingers, Jupiter in fact twists inwards leaning on domineering Saturn – relying heavily on the serious influence which controls Barry's deeper senses. This twist reveals some fundamental inadequacy and because of this people would be important to him, encouraging his potential and strength of purpose. The warp to Jupiter and the detachment of Mercury allies with the splitting of the head line (particularly clear on the left hand) to show a divided personality, a versatile, ever-changing character, accounting for his desire to assume different personalities. However, despite this split the head line looks compact and doesn't drop too far down into Neptune or Moon so this yen to adopt other roles is not necessarily fanatical or obsessional – remember that the birth hand is solid and square, keeping his personality under control! So his Dame Edna image, along with her dress sense, is ultimately prompted by the desire in his fingers rather than the true personality.

UPS AND DOWNS
The head line is slightly frayed and may account for his occasionally restless and finicky reactions. It commences low on mount Mars, a warlike start, full of assertiveness and energy, showing his mind's lively, passionate drive: an ability to fulfil both fantasies and practical plans. The irritability I detected here gives off a certain bohemian, abstract curiosity: he may find short, sharp experiences far more interesting than enduring, long term phases. I also sensed a lowering, dragging sensation to the line, bringing thoughts down to elementary levels, but internal strength is not sacrificed. He can raise his spirits from the lowest of the low (moods inspired by the clumsy lower palm and low-set head line) to the most sensational highs (reflected in the fanciful fingers and the gradual rise of the heart line towards Saturn, right hand).

NEW DIRECTIONS
The fate lines are not strong in these hands, indeed fate's intervention may have come about almost by accident,

probably by an unusual coincidence which ignited Barry's interest in accepting Destiny. Tracing the line on the left hand we can see a time of great joy around the age of 51 as it links with head and heart, a time to stand back and feel proud! Around 58 a major transformation in career looks inevitable, opening up new ground for Barry to explore. This is a time when the past can be laid to rest, but it's clear that this won't be easy for him since this fate influence is not evident in the right hand. He may find it hard to come to terms with the new routine and even try to divert it. Ups and downs early in life too: at the start of the fate line (age 17-18) I detected travel and some special influence over him; another inspiring time at about 21 soon followed by a major disappointment where a separation tears the heart line (and his soul) in two. This emotional wound doesn't start to heal until the end of his twenties, when a fresh, self-assertive start to a new life begins! As he turned 40 he was achieving some artistic and personal goal. The fifties are full of exhilarating new phases: the heart line has plenty of ambition in reserve for mature years – see the markings thrown off on to mount Jupiter revealing private dreams still brimming over with emotional enthusiasm.

These amazingly intriguing palms prove that Barry is led by a unique combination of three forces: expansive notions and fancies; a pugnacious driving spirit; a basic, earthy understanding of life. All three aspects roll into one full and awe-inspiring character who can be extraordinarily flamboyant in public but deep down is quite retreative and calm.

·P·R·O·F·I·L·E·

TV and radio personality

Date of Birth: 12 January 1933

Sun Sign: CAPRICORN

Element: Earth

Ruling Planet: Saturn

MICHAEL ASPEL

Reliable and resolute – that's Michael, with his broad, stable nails and knotted knuckles. There's strength and muscle revealed in his hands, and a quick mind and a common-sense approach to life. However, he's had to struggle to overcome an inherent weakness – a lurking shyness that chips away at his confidence. The carefree spacing of the fingers counteracts this, giving him an autonomy and self-sufficiency that can boldly take him where his retiring instincts might hesitate to go!

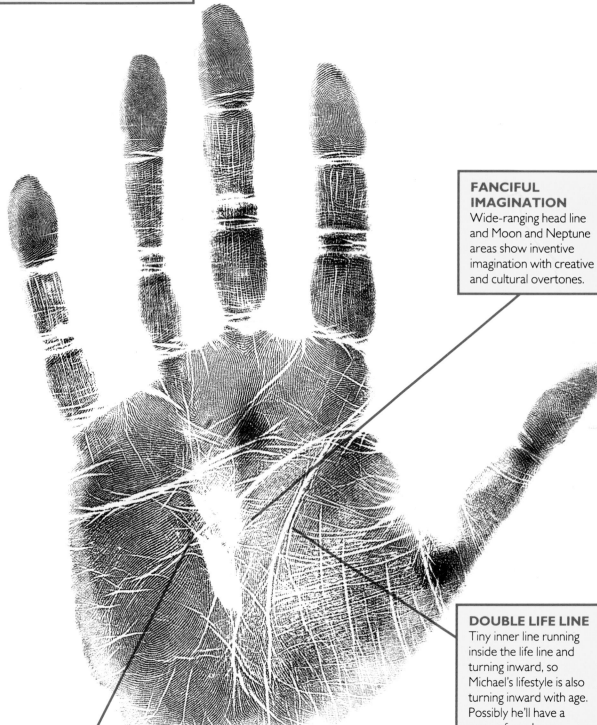

ARTISTIC FINGERTIPS
Refined oval-shaped tips appreciate beauty and elegance. He can relax and be refreshed by artistic interests.

FANCIFUL IMAGINATION
Wide-ranging head line and Moon and Neptune areas show inventive imagination with creative and cultural overtones.

DOUBLE LIFE LINE
Tiny inner line running inside the life line and turning inward, so Michael's lifestyle is also turning inward with age. Possibly he'll have a career from home, become more private? This impulse has been growing on him since his mid 30s. Compare fate line, right hand.

HEAD LINE
More sombre and confused than on right, showing past tendencies towards seriousness.

THE PAST HAND

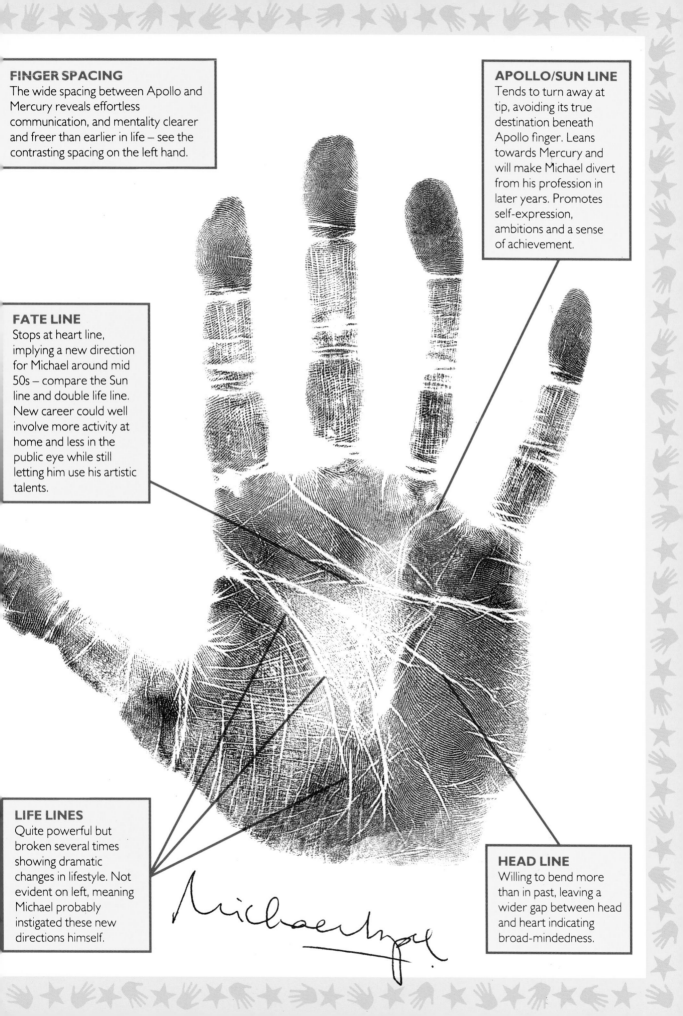

FINGER SPACING
The wide spacing between Apollo and Mercury reveals effortless communication, and mentality clearer and freer than earlier in life – see the contrasting spacing on the left hand.

APOLLO/SUN LINE
Tends to turn away at tip, avoiding its true destination beneath Apollo finger. Leans towards Mercury and will make Michael divert from his profession in later years. Promotes self-expression, ambitions and a sense of achievement.

FATE LINE
Stops at heart line, implying a new direction for Michael around mid 50s – compare the Sun line and double life line. New career could well involve more activity at home and less in the public eye while still letting him use his artistic talents.

LIFE LINES
Quite powerful but broken several times showing dramatic changes in lifestyle. Not evident on left, meaning Michael probably instigated these new directions himself.

HEAD LINE
Willing to bend more than in past, leaving a wider gap between head and heart indicating broad-mindedness.

SERIOUS SATURN

If Michael has managed to overcome his natural shyness it's through being hard on himself – you can see how the self-protective life line hugs the Venus mount showing the care and thoroughness with which he approaches any problem. This is underlined by the large Mercury fingers and strong head lines; together with the Venus mount (which I found very well defined when I manipulated the palms) they show how seriously he takes life – in fact his brain is so active and responsive to surroundings that he thinks too hard sometimes and can get confused. The head lines are rather thick and their slight unevenness bears out this occasional lack of focus. Unfortunately, being such a thinker, he probably sets his sights too high sometimes and finds himself quickly disillusioned.

INVENTIVE NEPTUNE

You can see a wide range of markings in the middle of the palms proving that Neptune is hard at work; Neptune inspires the graceful, poetic, mystical part of the imagination, the ability to write and think creatively. Michael is apt to fantasise, and might well lose himself in this false world if his innate practical side (which you can see in the squareness of the palms and the emphasis on logic in the long and free lower thumbs) did not bring him back down to earth. Of course, sometimes he does fly free – the Moon area is unusually large – but the serious, reflective side of his nature will always protect him when he gets carried away.

CHARISMATIC MERCURY

Look how wonderfully tall the Mercury and Apollo fingers are! No wonder Michael is so charismatic. Apollo of course enhances tolerance, love of beauty, people and culture; Mercury the ability to communicate on all levels, social, commercial and artistic. The distance between Apollo and Mercury (even discounting the slight warp to the Apollo finger which is due to a cricket injury) betrays a very slight aloofness; Michael likes to do things his own way. So in relationships, whether casual or serious, he probably demands a perfection that may be impossible to live up to. Mind you, it's equally impossible to avoid falling under the spell of his charm, which can be sensed in the beautifully silky texture of both palms! This delicacy implies that Michael's basic temperament is emotionally receptive and placid. But sexually, he's less placid, his mind is in control rather than his instincts, and if his partner is unresponsive then he'll react coldly (the heart line is short and low-set, implying low emotional energy). He needs the atmosphere to be right, for if his mind isn't inspired then his physical instincts won't be either. Nevertheless, there's a good breadth of feelings conveyed in the clear space between the fingers and the head and heart line.

The Sun/Apollo line starts on the heart line: as well as reinforcing Michael's charm, wit and dry sense of humour it indicates a great joy from emotional fulfilment during mid-life and onwards. In fact it's running off a second heart line which reveals a new surge of love – and indeed a new lease of life – later on. The charm will never die!

But there are undeniably dark clouds of moodiness amid the sunny charm. You can see how the head line is interrupted and broken in the middle of both palms where intense internal conflict lies, ready to resurrect any insecurities. But even if he has been misguided in the past, closing his eyes to reality, the right hand's fingers lean towards Jupiter, suggesting that he is more self-reliant now; self-respect and independent thinking have freed him from doubts. The head line in both hands desperately tries to detach itself from the life line, especially at the outset. Perhaps early in life, whether through insecurity or shyness, Michael found it hard to let go of people and places and trust to his own confidence? He's fought hard to shake off these clinging forces and as the head lines do succeed in breaking away we can see that Michael's powers of analysis *can* overcome his shyness. However much he may want to stay in the background that's just not going to happen!

CYNTHIA PAYNE

·P·R·O·F·I·L·E·

The famous Madam of Streatham

Date of Birth: 24 December 1932

Sun Sign: CAPRICORN

Element: Earth

Ruling Planet: Saturn

Madam Cyn's a fighter and a survivor with tiny yet courageous palms, firm delicate coating to the back of the hands, deeply-etched knuckles, short determined fingers and indulgent obsessive thumbs. These thumbs spread out well on the print but when you study them in the flesh they are more upright and nestle closely under the protection of the Jupiter fingers, which tells me she has steadfast and even moralistic attitudes, and she will fight for her rights to the bitter end.

A SHREWD SOUL

The head line is a good length showing that she can be shrewd, but it does not start on the hand at the point of birth so she may not be quick to grasp things initially. Yet the business sense is firm, she never forgets what she's learnt and can weigh things up intelligently. The line is lazy at the outset suggesting an awkward start at school, not much of a liking for academic pursuits, but since then she's developed the capacity to learn. This is an active soul who *should* be spiritually in tune and have a clear understanding of her life's tasks, but there are abnormalities

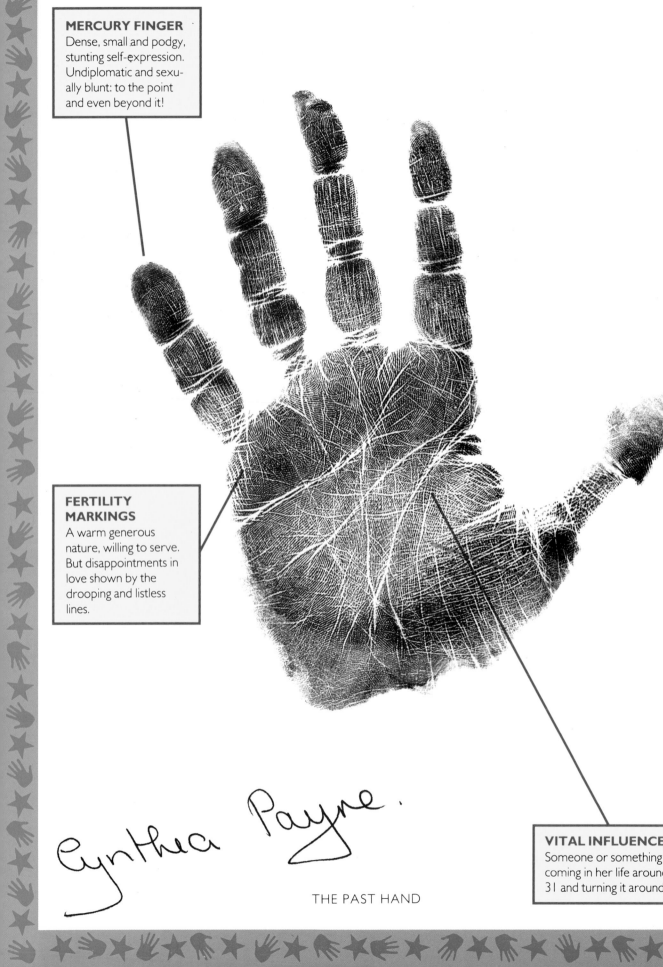

MERCURY FINGER
Dense, small and podgy, stunting self-expression. Undiplomatic and sexually blunt: to the point and even beyond it!

FERTILITY MARKINGS
A warm generous nature, willing to serve. But disappointments in love shown by the drooping and listless lines.

VITAL INFLUENCE
Someone or something coming in her life around 31 and turning it around.

THE PAST HAND

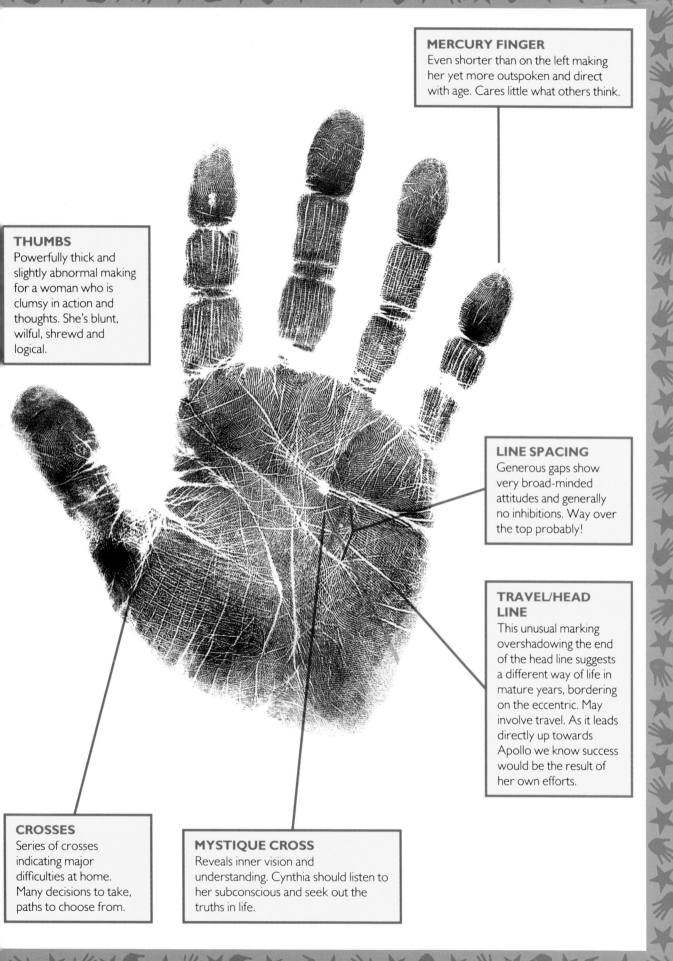

MERCURY FINGER
Even shorter than on the left making her yet more outspoken and direct with age. Cares little what others think.

THUMBS
Powerfully thick and slightly abnormal making for a woman who is clumsy in action and thoughts. She's blunt, wilful, shrewd and logical.

LINE SPACING
Generous gaps show very broad-minded attitudes and generally no inhibitions. Way over the top probably!

TRAVEL/HEAD LINE
This unusual marking overshadowing the end of the head line suggests a different way of life in mature years, bordering on the eccentric. May involve travel. As it leads directly up towards Apollo we know success would be the result of her own efforts.

CROSSES
Series of crosses indicating major difficulties at home. Many decisions to take, paths to choose from.

MYSTIQUE CROSS
Reveals inner vision and understanding. Cynthia should listen to her subconscious and seek out the truths in life.

that can lead her into false illusions. One thing's certain, she's got no regrets about her life nor any remorse, she uses any tumbles in life as a stepping stone on and upward.

NO HOLDS BARRED
Cynthia is strong willed: in fact she's got a stubborn streak a mile wide that eventually sways everyone into respecting her guts and staying power. This is clear from the way both thumbs are thick and short in a clumsy way, suggesting also a tactless and blunt approach to life that's reinforced by the strange shortness of the Mercury fingers. Indeed, such short Mercury digits encourage the coarser, uncultured aspects of the personality to surface so she *never* minds what she says. She's true to herself even if to others she appears unrefined or undignified. These two areas are where to look for her unconventional and flamboyant approach to sex. Look at the heart lines too – the marriage/relationship lines droop heavily towards them showing that she's suffered many a bitter emotional disappointment. But the heart lines themselves are deep, and thus more stable, despite their loops and detached areas, and retain all their vigour, generosity and possessiveness. Look at the generous spacing too, Cynthia is definitely broad-minded and uninhibited, and open to all manner of experiences, but however bizarre they haven't left a mark – she'll bounce back whatever.

THE OLDEST PROFESSION
So what about the sexuality? Mercury mount is covered with fertility markings. As this is the healing and giving area of the palm, it's from here she derives the willingness to please which encouraged her to become a madam, happy to cater to the whims and fantasies of others. She's tolerant and understanding and sensual – there's a flirtatious outline to the heart that's positively charismatic, and the mounts are earthy and fleshy. Venus is broad, sweeping its lusty energies across from the home front into the sexual sphere. She's a mixer and a socialiser. There's a mystical cross in the centre palm that reveals an intuition and compassion with which most people would not credit her. This receptive side to her nature shows she acts on impulse, following her basic instincts. Nearly all the fingertips are round suggesting she prefers an unusual lifestyle, an artistic one (though not artistic in the high-flown sense). In contrast the Jupiter tips are pointed which shows on one level that she needs to gather material possessions around her, and on another she needs to fulfil her idiosyncratic ideals and ambitions.

LIFE AT HOME
The life lines fluctuate in fits and starts, forging an uneven course through the years. Lots of stressful situations show up at the weakest points and only at the end do they fork, revealing good balance – eventually. There's an unusual curving back on itself at the mid 40s when Cynthia may have had to accept a dramatic change in lifestyle. Public interests take a back seat and the home life dominates again as the line strives to return to its home base. The influence of fate stems from the area of beauty, home and the social world – Venus – so it seems that she has a set route to follow, a career undertaken from home . . .

Although a woman of dubious reputation – undoubtedly disliked by some – you can't fail to fall under the spell of her charm and free spirit. I certainly did, when I met her, with my husband . . . on our wedding anniversary. I don't suppose many people can say they took their husband to a brothel as an anniversary celebration! But we found her friendly and outgoing and tenacious – you can admire her staunch perseverance however strange her goals appear. She's a home-loving creature, Venus and Moon never let her forget her maternal, earthbound instincts. Always in charge of her own life, whatever the cost. Her character may be rather unrefined but she genuinely cares – she never knows when to stop giving, or for that matter, fighting.

JAMES HERBERT

·P·R·O·F·I·L·E·

Author of 13 bestselling horror novels, including *The Rats*

Date of Birth: 8 April 1943

Sun Sign: ARIES

Element: Fire

Ruling Planet: Mars

I found these hands really fascinating. They are artistic yet serious and have a dramatic, mystical quality about them. They were complex yet intriguing because the lines are so erratic and the mounts so unbalanced.

REINCARNATED?

There are acute spiritual and psychic overtones here. James's hands are genteel, soft to touch and thickly covered with lines reinforcing the impression of a deeply perceptive man, open to everything around him. My spiritual intuition found an extremely 'old' look to both palms and this psychic feeling together with the complexity of the lines makes me sense that James has travelled on this earth before, possibly through many lifetimes. So we have a brimming, busy soul that's learning with each reincarnation but whose esoteric education is still not complete. I imagine James was master of many skills in his previous existences – maybe a teacher of them? – and now he is using them to the full. His soul is growing with each incarnation. There are two sides to this man: subdued and private – almost secretive – yet also extrovert.

HOLDING BACK

It must be very hard for someone with such a fragile, vulnerable nature to be in the public eye. James can't stop things affecting him and I daresay he instinctively puts up barriers to keep unwelcome outsiders at bay – and their criticism! You can see how the emotional area of both palms is very cluttered with lines, revealing someone governed by sensations and touch. Atmospheric conditions affect his health because he reacts emotionally to weather and temperature changes.

REACHING OUT

You can also see James's flair for communications by looking at the Venus and Mercury mounts: they are rounded and full, reflecting the outgoing side of his nature. The Venus particularly shows the passionate energy and singlemindedness James can put into his life at home or at social events. A sense of dedication and devotion really stretches him to the limit of his capabilities. He is idealistic and wholeheartedly enthusiastic about life, and about romantic and sexual behaviour – look at the broken and scattered girdle of Venus that swings out from beneath Mercury to Saturn. The energy he throws into life comes in fits and starts (see the irregular highs and lows of the mounts); James will spontaneously launch himself into projects, both physical and mental, but he undoubtedly runs out of steam very quickly.

SPIRITUAL DESTINY

I've mentioned the pronounced spiritual and psychic elements in the palms, which provide James with great inner knowledge. This, with the mystical air implied by the many small crosses in both palms, suggests that James's writing techniques are due to a force greater than his own. A spiritual teacher or guide working as a shadow alongside him would, I feel sure, encourage his inspiration and creativity. James belongs to a spiritual framework, with certain obligations to the unseen hierarchy. It is important therefore that he follows through on his life's plan and continues to do what is decreed for him.

The nails are shell-shaped and smallish, indicating that James has a tendency to a weaker constitution than most, although other areas on the hand can overcome this. Because the nails suggest worries about health in general, it is vital that James heeds his own body's signals when stress or tiredness takes over. He should watch his health particularly around the early fifties when a period of rest is indicated by the loop low on the life line. Just at the moment the tips of the fingers convey imbalance and he must take care now to relax when under undue pressure. Prints taken in a few months' time may well show the condition to be cleared.

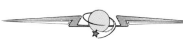

The day James came to my cottage was grey and angry, and since he is a writer of supernatural horror I rather expected to find him of a similarly ominous disposition. This was not the case! He came over as incredibly imaginative; a man who, although strong-willed and alert, can be quite soft. Nothing dark or sinister about him! I felt the spiritual connection immediately and am sure it inspires his writing. Don't be deceived by the tidy and methodical air to James's hands, he may take life seriously but I'm sure he has a little flippancy there which could creep out and surprise you!

LINES AND CROSSES

Very spiritual palms, thickly covered with lines – James is in tune with universal laws. Many crosses emphasise his intuition.

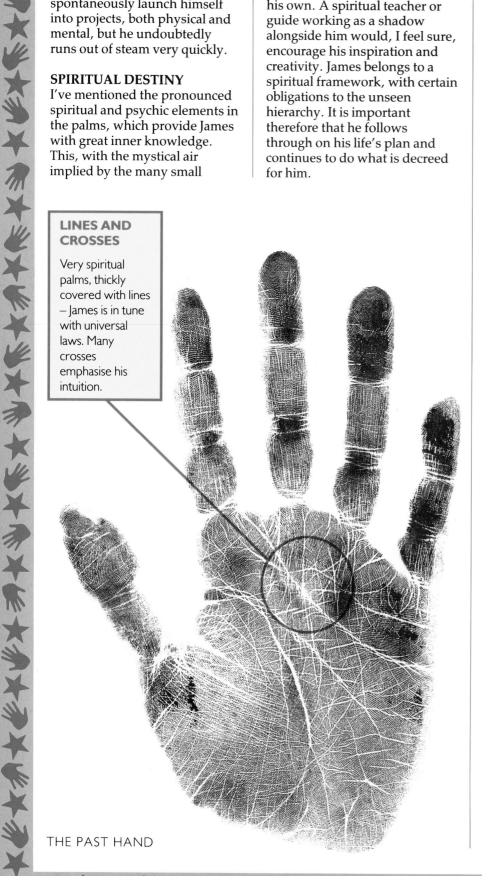

THE PAST HAND

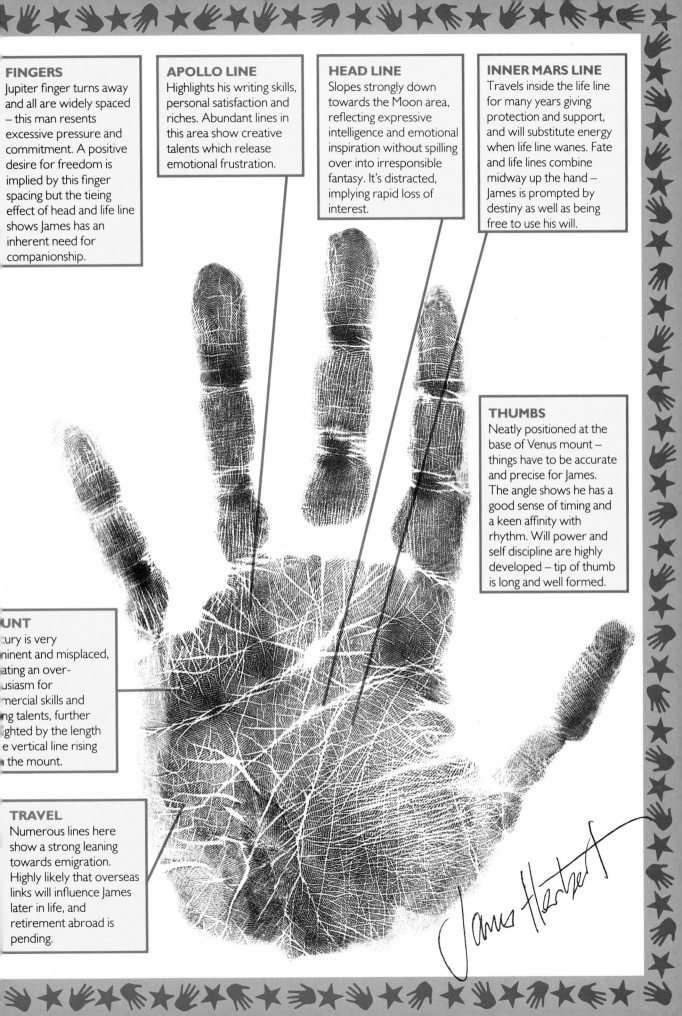

FINGERS
Jupiter finger turns away and all are widely spaced – this man resents excessive pressure and commitment. A positive desire for freedom is implied by this finger spacing but the tieing effect of head and life line shows James has an inherent need for companionship.

APOLLO LINE
Highlights his writing skills, personal satisfaction and riches. Abundant lines in this area show creative talents which release emotional frustration.

HEAD LINE
Slopes strongly down towards the Moon area, reflecting expressive intelligence and emotional inspiration without spilling over into irresponsible fantasy. It's distracted, implying rapid loss of interest.

INNER MARS LINE
Travels inside the life line for many years giving protection and support, and will substitute energy when life line wanes. Fate and life lines combine midway up the hand – James is prompted by destiny as well as being free to use his will.

THUMBS
Neatly positioned at the base of Venus mount – things have to be accurate and precise for James. The angle shows he has a good sense of timing and a keen affinity with rhythm. Will power and self discipline are highly developed – tip of thumb is long and well formed.

...UNT
...cury is very ...minent and misplaced, ...ating an over-...usiasm for ...mercial skills and ...ng talents, further ...ighted by the length ...e vertical line rising ...the mount.

TRAVEL
Numerous lines here show a strong leaning towards emigration. Highly likely that overseas links will influence James later in life, and retirement abroad is pending.

SUE COOK

·P·R·O·F·I·L·E·

TV presenter, including
Crimewatch UK

Date of Birth: 30 March 1949

Sun Sign: ARIES

Element: Fire

Ruling Planet: Mars

S ue's hands look soft and dreamy with their long, elegant fingers, but a closer inspection reveals her to be both sensible and confident. While we are quite falsely supposing her to be fanciful and feminine she's actually breathtakingly independent and self-sufficient – look at the line spacing! Here's stamina and enthusiasm, the ability to cope easily with setbacks.

BRIGHT AND BEGUILING

Sue draws people to her with her gentle charm but she'd not let herself become another's possession – they'd have to respect her need for space and independence. This is an inherited trait.

She trusts people readily and has a high regard for the human race, but there's shyness deep down that can make her self-respect waver, implicit in the relative shortness of the Jupiter fingers. Everything else in the palms leans towards confidence, a trait seen right from birth. Her palms are very pliable with outer smoothness suggesting that self-expression and outward appearance matter to her – but not so pliable as to make her vulnerable for she retains her self-assurance. A neat balance, for overly supple hands tend to let others rule, something Sue could not tolerate. Her long tapering fingers and wide palms reveal fanciful notions and creativity mixed with logic and materialism. Sue's palms are conic/artistic showing an appreciation of beauty and talent, and intuitive responses. The sharp dip in the head line could prompt sudden mood changes and a hatred of boring routine. She wears a large dark ring on the Saturn finger which reinforces this forward-moving energy, and accentuates her strong-mindedness. But it could never hide the fragility that makes her such a warm, appealing person.

A FINE ROMANCER

Sue's probably not aware of this, but she takes the lead in most situations, quietly but firmly. This is undoubtedly true in personal relationships, within which she has very high standards and morals. This orderliness is reflected in the way Saturn leans toward Apollo. She's a perfectionist in romance, and will watch people carefully before committing herself. She's not often wrong for she has an instant rapport with people and an unfailing sense of judgement born of her inner sensitivity. But naturally she sometimes gets attached too easily. She'd hate to hurt others, but unfortunately the dreaminess we've already picked out can make her blunder clumsily when fantasy clouds the rose-tinted spectacles she sometimes dons. Sue's a creative woman who needs romance – see the possessive heart line – but she likes to be in control.

PETER PAN APPEAL

There's an extraordinary youthfulness to Sue's nature, a freshness and a purity: almost Peter Pan-like! But the dreams can get away from her, just as the head line forces its way down into the Moon area. She's influenced deeply by Neptune (note the busyness in the centre palms) and is in tune with the cosmos. The harmony of nature and spiritual forces make her calm and happy. Her soul heals very rapidly – Sue thinks ahead and leaves ills behind, always clearing the ground for the future. She has the patience to work with youth, to nurture and encourage them, while at the same time being hard on herself. This may keep her vision pure and her identity intact but I'm afraid it makes her lose out on a lot of fun.

We've all seen Sue on the TV, perhaps we should be seeing her in print? For the head line, long and sloping creatively into Moon, insists that Sue could be good at writing. The beautiful, graceful curve to this line encourages artistic endeavours while the fork at the end not only unfetters her whimsical imagination, it lets her see both sides of any situation. So we've come full circle – here's a balance between her dreamy creativity on the one side, and on the other, her notable intelligence.

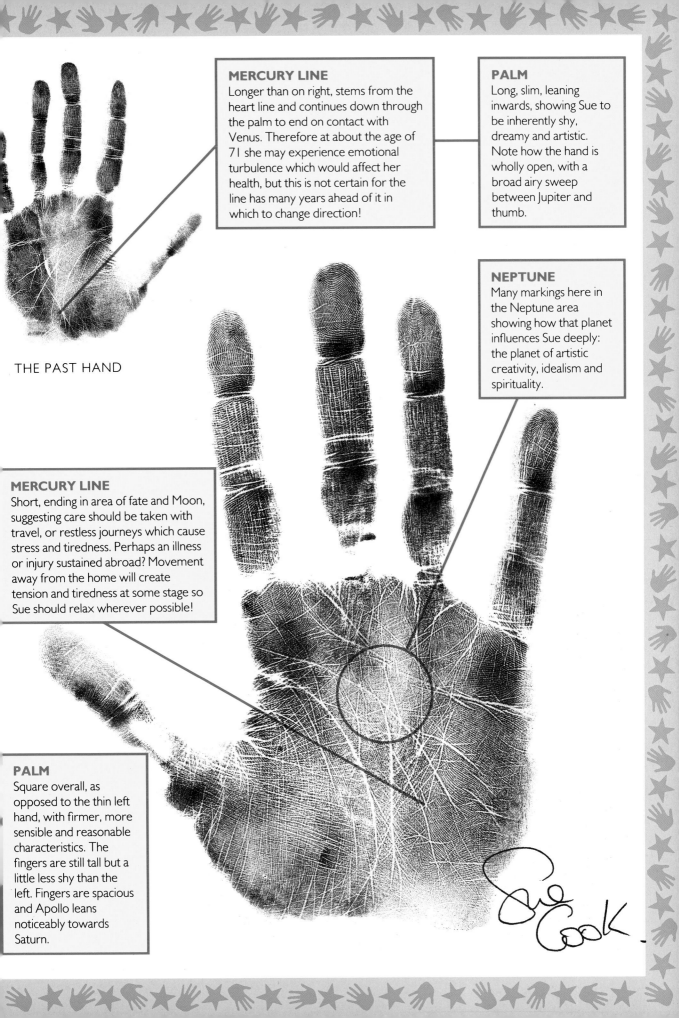

MERCURY LINE
Longer than on right, stems from the heart line and continues down through the palm to end on contact with Venus. Therefore at about the age of 71 she may experience emotional turbulence which would affect her health, but this is not certain for the line has many years ahead of it in which to change direction!

PALM
Long, slim, leaning inwards, showing Sue to be inherently shy, dreamy and artistic. Note how the hand is wholly open, with a broad airy sweep between Jupiter and thumb.

THE PAST HAND

NEPTUNE
Many markings here in the Neptune area showing how that planet influences Sue deeply: the planet of artistic creativity, idealism and spirituality.

MERCURY LINE
Short, ending in area of fate and Moon, suggesting care should be taken with travel, or restless journeys which cause stress and tiredness. Perhaps an illness or injury sustained abroad? Movement away from the home will create tension and tiredness at some stage so Sue should relax wherever possible!

PALM
Square overall, as opposed to the thin left hand, with firmer, more sensible and reasonable characteristics. The fingers are still tall but a little less shy than the left. Fingers are spacious and Apollo leans noticeably towards Saturn.

GLORIA HUNNIFORD

·P·R·O·F·I·L·E·

TV and radio personality

Date of Birth: 10 April 1940

Sun Sign: ARIES

Element: Fire

Ruling Planet: Mars

Gloria is vivacious, energetic and self-assertive, blessed with a pioneering spirit. This is reflected in the dominant features of her hands: prominent mounts, generous fleshy areas at the base of the fingers and dry and firm skin. The lengthy Mercury finger and equally strong head lines show that she has an extremely sharp and intuitive mind and a dry sense of humour – in fact a rather mischievous personality. Often seeing the funny side helps her retain an optimistic approach to life. These hands look neat and self-contained, reflecting order and precision within. Gloria does not always follow convention and there is a slightly rebellious streak running through her wide-open, free-thinking fingers. She may defy organised plans and even tempt fate itself at times! These hands belong to a hard worker, but one who may analyse projects and ventures too much. The wide Venus area together with the many 'people' lines tell us that she takes pride in herself and also in her work. Social and domestic spheres, and career, are all equally important to her. Inspiration, wit and a good memory feature here – but tact may be lacking at times! You can see her cheeky determination

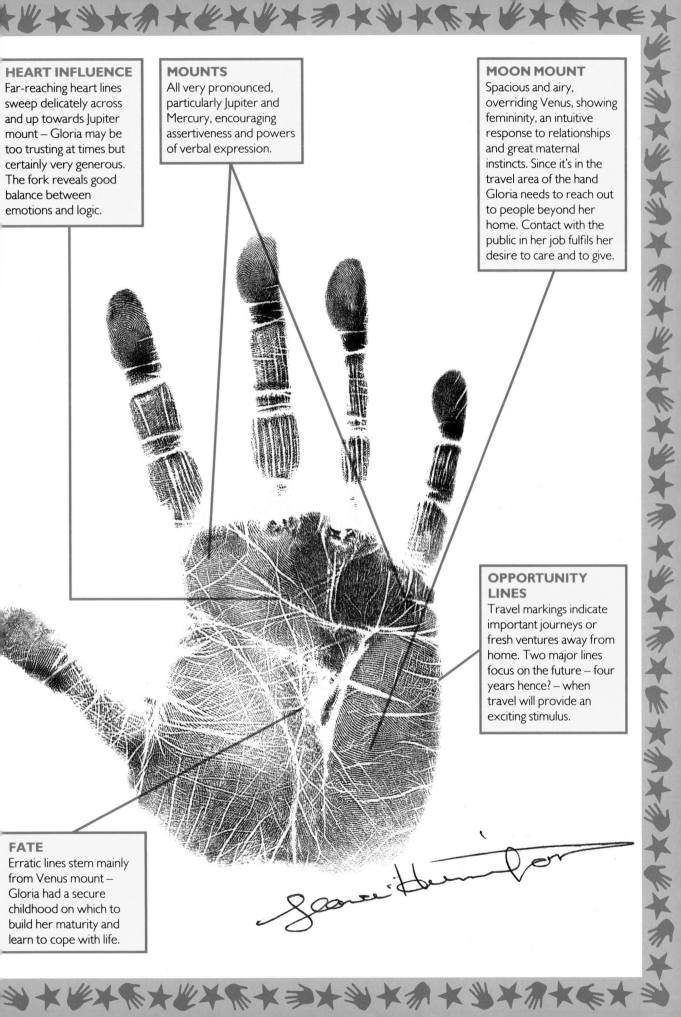

HEART INFLUENCE
Far-reaching heart lines sweep delicately across and up towards Jupiter mount – Gloria may be too trusting at times but certainly very generous. The fork reveals good balance between emotions and logic.

MOUNTS
All very pronounced, particularly Jupiter and Mercury, encouraging assertiveness and powers of verbal expression.

MOON MOUNT
Spacious and airy, overriding Venus, showing femininity, an intuitive response to relationships and great maternal instincts. Since it's in the travel area of the hand Gloria needs to reach out to people beyond her home. Contact with the public in her job fulfils her desire to care and to give.

OPPORTUNITY LINES
Travel markings indicate important journeys or fresh ventures away from home. Two major lines focus on the future – four years hence? – when travel will provide an exciting stimulus.

FATE
Erratic lines stem mainly from Venus mount – Gloria had a secure childhood on which to build her maturity and learn to cope with life.

reflected in the palms but there is an element of risk-taking which means that actions can result in clumsy blunders if not thought out and better timed.

A LOGICAL LADY

There are broken lines around the logic area (base of the thumb, second phalange) especially where this phalange links into mount Venus, implying that Gloria will absorb information carefully and analyse it, always seeking the logical, organised solution. She has a keen sense of priorities. Her thumbs (which govern the ego and will, ruling the ability to assert oneself) are both long and versatile, revealing vitality and healthy self esteem. There is confidence here and if you add this to the wide spacing of fingers and of head and heart line you see a glowing example of a woman in command of her life, one who can hold on to her ideals and standards when disillusioned.

MIND OVER MATTER

The good thumb, strong lean head line and tall Mercury fingers mean that this lady is very much in charge of her own mind. She acts spontaneously, following her instincts and psychic power, but is almost invariably in control – and any opposition is dealt with by her sharp wit! Gloria's determined mind drives her forward, making her an enterprising, energetic character. Mars is her ruling planet and is the main incentive behind her personality. We can see from all this that inner strength, superiority and decisiveness dominate in these irrepressible, aggressive hands. Mercury and Jupiter influence the mind too, and all these areas of the hand are emphasised, suggesting heightened mental perception. She can fight her own battles, yet still come out looking fresh and fit for the next bout. Mental tenacity is a bonus here.

Eloquent and on the ball, Gloria always gets straight to the heart of the matter and has no qualms about putting her point of view across to others! The encouraging spacing, not only between her fingers but between all of the lines on the hand, make her uninhibited, broad-minded, open and honest. She will try anything once, in fact she could well become a glutton for new and exciting adventures – anything for a challenge.

SENSE...

Gloria is very sensitive, but the firm texture of her skin shows that her feelings can be well supervised and disciplined. I'd say though, that she tends towards vulnerability. The high-set heart line shows an idealistic, romantic attitude and high standards in the emotional area of life, highlighting her femininity.

... AND SEXUALITY

From a sexual point of view Gloria is once again adventurous: lovemaking must be exciting and sensual. However, as she is a romantic at heart, tenderness isn't sacrificed for passion. Look at the delicately-curved heart lines, reaching up towards the mount of Jupiter, showing loyalty to others. But you'll see from the way they fail to connect completely with the fingers that there might be a slight lack of obligation. Although I feel there are other major passions that could motivate Gloria and be equally satisfying, there is a sexual spontaneity (seen in the good round Moon area, high heart line and gentle arched girdle of Venus) which comes bounding through, showing that she can respond pretty rapidly to sexual advances. But she must beware of putting people on pedestals and being deluded into a false interpretation of their motives.

The continuous, restless, fine markings visible all over the palms indicate the possibility of past lives. In a previous incarnation Gloria would no doubt have had strong overseas links. She may well have been a sportsperson with a love of travel, someone constantly on the move. I can't help feeling slightly envious of Gloria, of her staying power, her enthusiasm and drive. She knows where she stands in life, she values her responsibilities and she has the capacity to fulfil all her ambitions.

DEREK JAMESON

·P·R·O·F·I·L·E·

Radio presenter, TV personality,
ex-Fleet Street editor

Date of Birth: 29 November 1929

Sun Sign: SAGITTARIUS

Element: Fire

Ruling Planet: Jupiter

Derek's two hands are
very different, and
testify to the way he has
changed over the years.

**EVERYTHING VENTURED,
EVERYTHING GAINED**
Derek is left-handed, so to delve
into his past you have to look at
his right hand where you'll see a
free-spirited personality with
openly-spaced fingers and lines.

But on his progressive (left)
hand that element of risk-taking
is modified; the fingers and lines
lie closer together. Derek has
become more direct, upright and
moralistic, and stronger; a
personality tempered by
experience. Look at the
unusually short and impulsive
head line on the right hand –
Derek used to jump head first
into situations without thinking.
But then look at the difference
on the left hand: there it's
more normal, better controlled

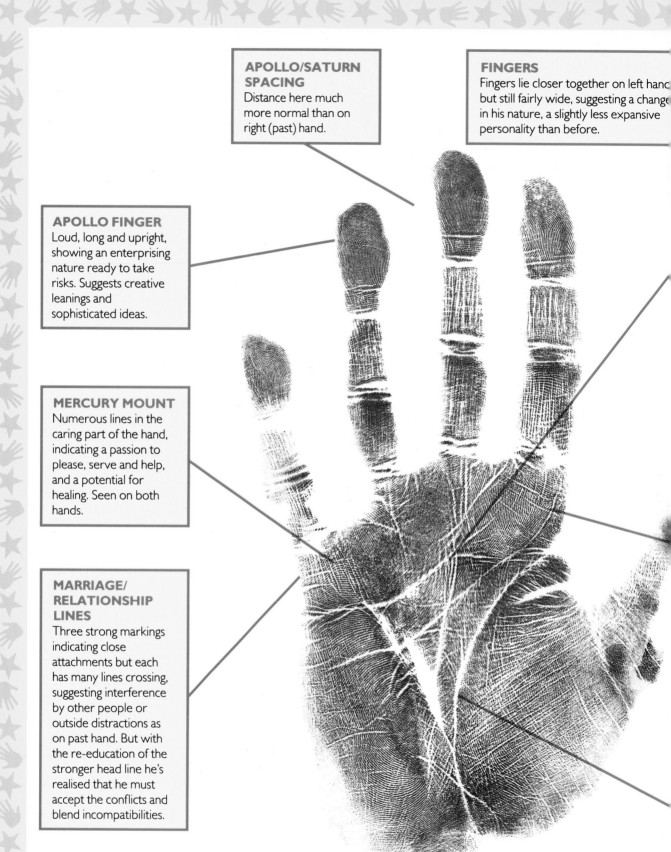

APOLLO/SATURN SPACING
Distance here much more normal than on right (past) hand.

FINGERS
Fingers lie closer together on left hand but still fairly wide, suggesting a change in his nature, a slightly less expansive personality than before.

APOLLO FINGER
Loud, long and upright, showing an enterprising nature ready to take risks. Suggests creative leanings and sophisticated ideas.

MERCURY MOUNT
Numerous lines in the caring part of the hand, indicating a passion to please, serve and help, and a potential for healing. Seen on both hands.

MARRIAGE/ RELATIONSHIP LINES
Three strong markings indicating close attachments but each has many lines crossing, suggesting interference by other people or outside distractions as on past hand. But with the re-education of the stronger head line he's realised that he must accept the conflicts and blend incompatibilities.

[HE]ART LINE

[Com]pare the line on the right hand
[whic]h is very long, loyal, warm and
[gene]rous. It is still full of these qualities
[in hi]s current hand but there's a split
[indic]ating some dramatic interference.
[The] girdle of Venus above is trying to
[smoo]th out the emotional problem by
[fusi]ng with the heart line, and in times
[like t]hese, lines may well blend and
[go b]ack to the original shape as on the
[right] hand.

HEAD LINE

Very long, thoughtful
and serious,
commencing right up on
Jupiter mount – his
dreams will never be
shattered! It shows he's
developed true
intelligence and the
capacity to think
logically. Compare the
right hand where it's
extremely short and
bombastic, not even
beginning at the birth
area.

[LIF]E LINE

[Man]y lines encroaching on it showing
[how] much people affect Derek. Fate
[line] protects it, helping him put aside
[the] gripings of life. The line hugs close
[to V]enus showing possessiveness.
[Thic]k and clumsy in first half – some
[pro]blems and/or blunders in life,
[set]tings in personal affairs – but from
[the] 40s on it's a more normal depth –
[pro]blems have been sorted out.
[Thi]ckness implies digestive imbalance
[so] Derek needs to watch his diet.

and longer; graceful, thoughtful
and serious. There's been a
major character transformation:
Derek's pulled his socks up!
What he's lost in impulsiveness
and daring over the years he's
gained in sense and
understanding of life.

FÊTED BY FATE

He does have marvellously
pliant hands, suggesting a very
adaptable and versatile nature. It
also implies robust health. And
most of all they're lucky hands
that really give value for money
– Derek will always land on his
feet!

Many people consider
themselves or others to be lucky;
such people often have a fate
line like Derek's, running
protectively parallel to his life
line. But is this luck? Can it not
imply that he's been strongly
influenced either by an unseen
guide or by Destiny? You can see
particularly in the right hand
that fate will have counteracted
his natural recklessness – even
when he jumped into things
with his eyes closed fate made
sure of a happy ending. So, he
could be sheltered by a spiritual
force. Fate, Spirit, Lady Luck –
call it what you will – this is the
driving element behind him, a
quality strengthened by his
ability to remain detached from
material nuisances and retreat
from the world when necessary.
I felt that he is acutely attuned to
the flow of cosmic energy.

A COMPLEX MAN

On his present hand the life line
hugs Venus and the heart line is
very deep, showing
possessiveness and a need to
belong. He puts up with things
in a way he would not have done
in the past. There's a rather lazy,
carefree attitude about his hands
now that slows him down. You
can see it in the setting of the
thumb and its uninterrupted
shape, and the heavy, rather
clumsy nature of the hands. But
he's also ambitious and his inner

drive is provided by the long and
willowy Jupiter finger on the left
hand that promotes dreams and
schemes. His ability to take ideas
and translate them into reality is
reinforced by the Jupiterian
qualities of the upright thumb
and large Jupiter finger. I noticed
some physical tiredness at the
moment and I think Derek
should heed his body's
limitations and balance work,
rest and play carefully. That he
has a very sensitive nervous
system is obvious – look at the
network of lines rising from
Venus to the Saturn area,
showing that he responds
readily to atmosphere and
conditions surrounding him.
He's a man who needs to keep
all the strands of his life in
balance.

I found signs indicating three
major career changes in the
progressive (left) hand – new
paths to follow probably in his
late 50s and early 60s. There are
lots of travel lines on both palms
that suggest he needs change:
not necessarily abroad, but not
staying in the same old rut.
When these kinds of lines
appear on the Moon mount
you'll find an enquiring mind
that needs to explore and be
constantly refreshed. New
experiences make him
appreciate life all the more so
there's no doubt Derek should
be blessed with lots of energy for
the years to come.

FINGERS
Wide spacing shows independence, self-sufficiency and a need for freedom and excitement.

APOLLO/SATURN SPACING
Strange distance here revealing a time in the past when Derek followed his instincts and impulses rather than reality and rational thought.

APOLLO FINGER
Tall and straight, as on left hand; shows no fear of challenges or attempting the unusual. Longs to reach people. Bulbous shape shows impulsive action and speech, clumsy and blunt approach to projects and people.

MERCURY MOUNT
Healing potential in the lines here could be fulfilled through Derek's job as he amuses people and encourages them to forget themselves and their problems.

MARRIAGE/RELATIONSHIP LINES
Strong lines disrupted by markings crossing, indicating that Derek would need an understanding partner to put up with all the outside nosiness. Disruption appears on current hand too. Interfering lines indicate importance of possessions.

HEAD LINE
Very different from the left hand. Starts late and stops short, showing impulsiveness, lack of tact and forethought, clumsiness.

THE PAST HAND

FERN BRITTON

·P·R·O·F·I·L·E·

Co-presenter of TVS's *Coast to Coast* with Fred Dinenage

Date of Birth: 17 July 1957

Sun Sign: CANCER

Element: Water

Ruling Planet: Moon

These hands can cope with almost anything or anyone. They are large, round, even masculine, yet very flexible with sensitive skin. Their plump fleshiness implies indefatigability but there are vulnerable areas around the Moon and Venus mounts which affect not only Fern's health but her spirits too.

A LOVE AFFAIR WITH LIFE

Moon is her ruling planet and it's a changeable one, as is her personality – see the well-defined, searching markings on the expansive mount Venus. The mount's sweeping effect shows also emotional receptiveness; full of warmth and passion, she needs to be loved and wanted and admired. In fact she's in love with life itself! She is intensely loyal but sometimes naive. Since the planets also affect our health, and Venus in particular rules the throat, upper chest and lumbar regions, she probably has a tendency to coughs and colds and aches and pains which should not be ignored. Fern should try and avoid irritations in life which upset her because her emotions affect her health, particularly with the added influence of the Moon. The palms are longer than the fingers showing how intensely she reacts to earthly passions; this quality is again emphasised by the large Moon and Venus mounts.

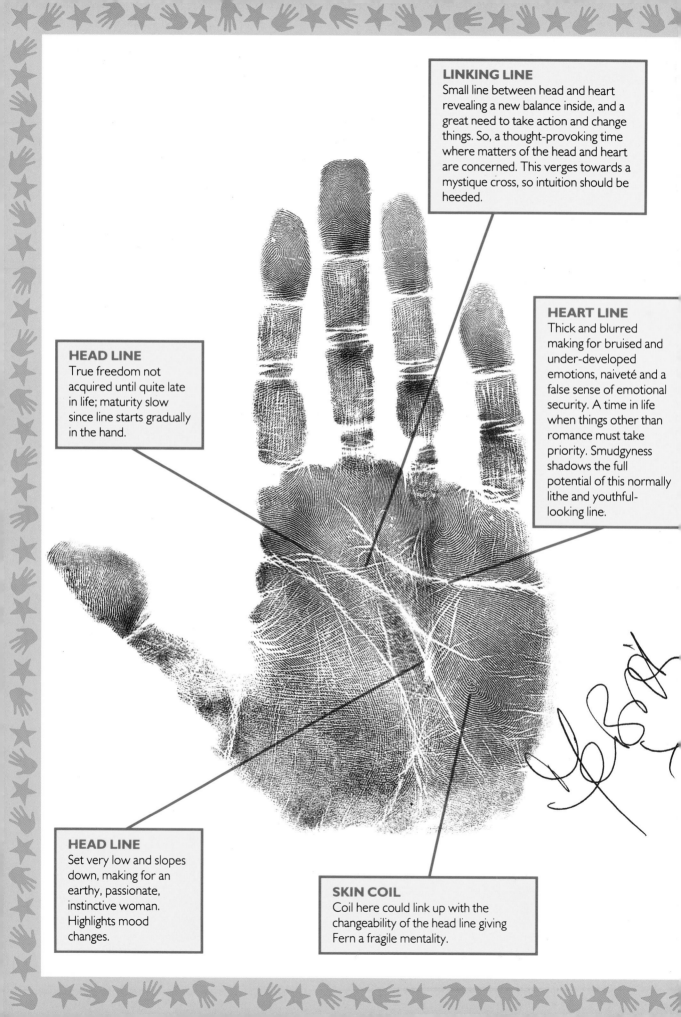

LINKING LINE
Small line between head and heart revealing a new balance inside, and a great need to take action and change things. So, a thought-provoking time where matters of the head and heart are concerned. This verges towards a mystique cross, so intuition should be heeded.

HEAD LINE
True freedom not acquired until quite late in life; maturity slow since line starts gradually in the hand.

HEART LINE
Thick and blurred making for bruised and under-developed emotions, naiveté and a false sense of emotional security. A time in life when things other than romance must take priority. Smudgyness shadows the full potential of this normally lithe and youthful-looking line.

HEAD LINE
Set very low and slopes down, making for an earthy, passionate, instinctive woman. Highlights mood changes.

SKIN COIL
Coil here could link up with the changeability of the head line giving Fern a fragile mentality.

SLOW BUT SURE

The roundness of both palms, and the awkward finger shapings, insinuate that Fern has a lazy side to her – 'ambling' is a word that springs to mind – but there's still tenacity of spirit and enough vitality to cope with life. She's a competitor who thrives on challenges, but she won't be hurried beyond her own rather plodding pace, nor be diverted from her cause. All this is reflected in the way the head lines fail to start at the time of birth (at the edge of the palm): they're most definitely slow off the mark.

HOME IS WHERE THE HEART IS

The lower phalanges are plump, which together with the fullness of her hands and the wide mount Venus make the social and domestic areas of life important to her. She loves nature, pets, gardening and cooking. She must be a good hostess (her wide sweeping life line shows how friendly and sociable she is) but perhaps an untidy one (remember the lazy signs)! The home environment is where Fern can relax most, especially with a pet or two. Animals are great healers and because of her Moon qualities she would find them a calming influence, for the Moon brings out a desire to touch and cherish.

There's a conflict in the hand between the desire for friendship and involvement and the need for solitude and quiet. The former is denoted by the fingers leaning together and the outgoing life line, while the latter is seen in the long Saturn finger, the wide spacing of all the lines and the low set head line, where sombre qualities surface. Fern needs to be noticed as an individual and as a self-sufficient woman but the Moon's influence creates a bubbling inferno beneath the cool exterior.

DRAMA IN DAILY LIFE

Touch is important to Fern, as is passion and romance: look at the round fleshy hands, the prominent Venus and Moon mounts. These also show how she's drawn to vibrant colours and aromas and inspired by them – and how astonishingly her imagination can run riot. Her emotions carry her along a dramatic path, full of thrilling peaks and stressful troughs, for deep passion can be a torment at times. The position of Moon and Venus in these hands give Fern deep feminine and maternal tendencies which mean she reacts emotionally to other people and is open to everything around her.

The heart line is a little thick and clustered, suggesting that sometimes romance has to be pushed aside so other areas of her life can blossom. But on the whole it's well-balanced, neatly forking at the Saturn mount, giving her good control over her deepest feelings. Close relationships can be deceptive and I expect Fern may not discover certain truths about her partners until after she's committed herself.

MOON MOODS AND VIVID VISIONS

There's an almost neurotic set to the head line because it dips so deeply to the base of Moon, which together with the width of this mount shows that Fern's imagination is so fertile that it can lose itself in unreality; that in her search for perfection she lets her powers of reason get out of control. So her liveliness of mind unfortunately has a darker side. She swings from the highest of highs to the lowest of lows. Although affected by outside conditions and other people there's no real rhyme nor reason to these mood swings apart from a basic vulnerability and the fluctuating 28-day cycle of the Moon. This propensity to drift into the realms of fantasy can be

a bonus if used positively, but if left running amok it's a negative force; terribly destructive and frightening, heralding a complete loss of grip on reality. Fern should switch off to those things that make her worry so.

I mentioned laziness earlier; it's reiterated by the slow start to the head line. She must have suffered these fluctuations in brain power even during childhood.

And what about the future? If you look at the heart line you'll see it's rather thick and obstructive just below the mount of Mercury: the emotions aren't running freely through a clear line, so affairs of the heart won't flourish just now. It'd be best to burn up these passions somewhere else for the time being. Thirty-three, however, sees an upswing leading on to lots of good things. So early to mid 30s emotions are riding high (although sometimes erratically) in contrast to the rather worn-out feeling at the moment where the heart and head lines blur. This made me wonder if the emotions have been misused recently? The smudgy effect to the heart line looks as if it's desperately trying to wipe out memories from the past. There's a line linking the head and heart just below the Saturn mount showing that 30 to 31 is the time for Fern to change her lifestyle. There's a special meeting to be seen at about the age of 33 – a new person overriding another in her life. This is indicated by the two lines travelling inside the life line. So, closing on a comfortable thought, Fern can be sure of support for five to eight years to come.

FRED DINENAGE

·P·R·O·F·I·L·E·

Co-presenter of TVS's *Coast to Coast* with Fern Britton

Date of Birth: 8 June 1942

Sun Sign: GEMINI

Element: Air

Ruling Planet: Mercury

Here we have the large, rounded, effusive palms of an immensely adaptable and energetic man who's flexible enough to get involved with many different projects at once, while thinking about something completely different at the same time!

LIVELY LIFESTYLE

Fred is ruled by the powerful planet Mercury which means he can push and push himself to extremes. Combining this with the animated head line and the great mental and physical activity in the overall palm (the physicality being reflected in the size of the palm when compared to the fingers) Fred is an intensely quick-thinking and quick-acting man. He has the rather elastic mentality associated with a sensitive nature but his hyperactivity can make him nervous and indeed when I touched his palms they were clammy, reflecting his fidgetiness.

BRAIN DRAINED

The head line is long and alluring showing an enquiring mind. Fred is curious and analytical but the rounded outside palms may make him avoid the logical route at times. You can see the impulsiveness in the strong-willed tip of the thumbs and their length. He constantly questions and may well be annoyed by rules and regulations for he has an innate independence. His mind tends to work overtime and probably tires him out with its ceaseless investigating and planning. Mercury plays havoc with the head line, exaggerating the importance of thoughts, communication and self-expression in Fred's life. It cuts directly across the palm reflecting a direct thought flow; that is, Fred has a methodical brain that can follow things through. It's also very deep; it must drain his energy and leave him subdued and serious. Physical exercise is a marvellous way of clearing the head of unwanted frustrations – so on yer bike, Fred!

Mercury, his ruling planet, blesses him with sound judgement, a sense of humour and a bubbly personality. The Mercury finger is very long; this, with the dominant head line, is where Fred's powers of communication come from.

PLIANT PERSONALITY

Both palms are extremely flexible, denoting a weakness for getting roped into things without second thoughts. So, we can add gullibility to the list with inquisitiveness, receptiveness and intuition! These hands are open and easily manipulated showing freedom but also restlessness.

LADY LUCK

Look at the enormous number of people and involvement lines crossing mount Venus, showing his love of others. The heart lines flit across the palms reflecting the light-hearted side to his character and a certain flirtatiousness. People attach themselves readily to him, attracted by his wit and enigmatic charm, but the light-hearted outward nature that draws others to him can sometimes raise a barrier between them and his real feelings. The lower half of the palms (the material and physical sphere) conveys a practical side that loves luxuries – clothes, travel, food, art and good living. This earthiness is emphasised yet further at the broad base of the palms.

All along the life line small lines break off upwards: these are 'incentive' markings, revealing goodness, progress and lucky breaks in life.

The fate line runs strongly and directly across the centre of the palm, showing that Fred tends to be governed by Destiny. It stems from the Moon mount so public life was ordained for him from the start. But it does not exert its influence until quite late (age 27–30). Now, mid 40s, fate is preparing him for more changes: it's an unpredictable period. But don't despair, there are uplifting times at 44, 45, 47 and 52: no need to worry about fate's interception here because these changes will result only in success.

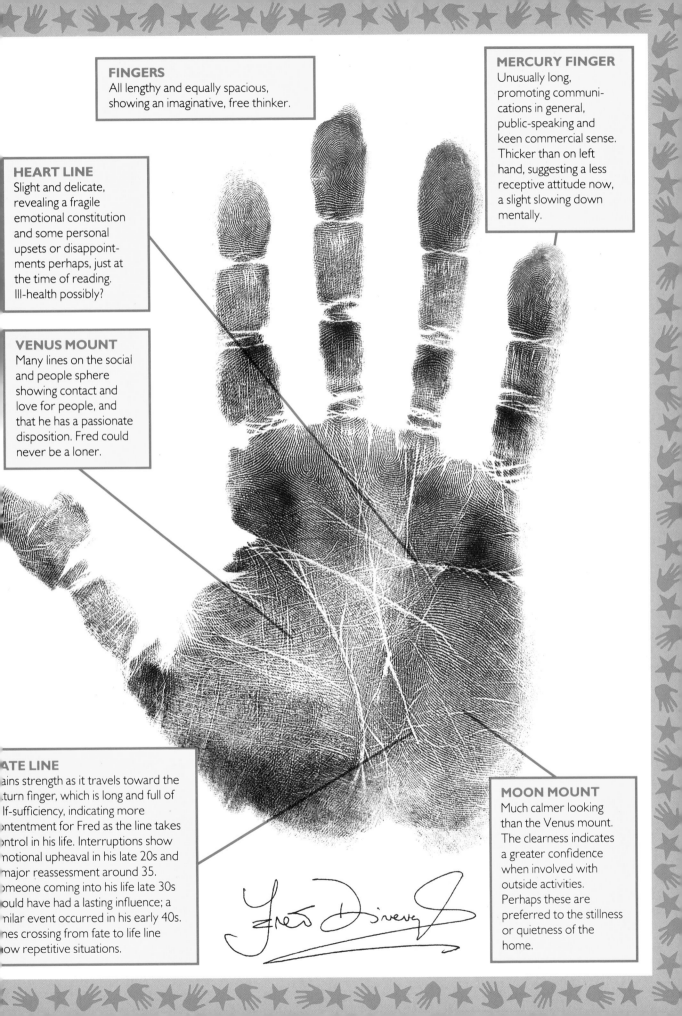

FINGERS
All lengthy and equally spacious, showing an imaginative, free thinker.

MERCURY FINGER
Unusually long, promoting communications in general, public-speaking and keen commercial sense. Thicker than on left hand, suggesting a less receptive attitude now, a slight slowing down mentally.

HEART LINE
Slight and delicate, revealing a fragile emotional constitution and some personal upsets or disappointments perhaps, just at the time of reading. Ill-health possibly?

VENUS MOUNT
Many lines on the social and people sphere showing contact and love for people, and that he has a passionate disposition. Fred could never be a loner.

ATE LINE
ains strength as it travels toward the turn finger, which is long and full of lf-sufficiency, indicating more ontentment for Fred as the line takes ontrol in his life. Interruptions show motional upheaval in his late 20s and major reassessment around 35. omeone coming into his life late 30s ould have had a lasting influence; a milar event occurred in his early 40s. nes crossing from fate to life line ow repetitive situations.

MOON MOUNT
Much calmer looking than the Venus mount. The clearness indicates a greater confidence when involved with outside activities. Perhaps these are preferred to the stillness or quietness of the home.

BERYL REID O.B.E.

·P·R·O·F·I·L·E·

Actress

Date of Birth: 17 June

Sun Sign: GEMINI

Element: Air

Ruling Planet: Mercury

O f all the hands I studied for this book, Beryl's were probably the most unusual and difficult for me to assess because arthritis has distorted their natural shape, making the fingers lean rather erratically. As Beryl puts it, 'they've been knocked about a bit.' However, when I looked at her hands it was immediately obvious that the fingers dominate, with Jupiter, Saturn and Apollo taking command, for the lines on the palm are lazy – almost weak – making way for the desires of the fingers to rule. Then, when I held Beryl's hands, the palms were so soft and silky to touch that I felt the skin would break under the slightest pressure. She obviously has a super-sensitive disposition and probably overreacts to things.

A CRAVING FOR CELEBRITY

You only have to look at the unusual length of the Apollo (Sun) finger and the equally tall Saturn finger to know that here's someone who puts personal fulfilment very high on her list of priorities. The long Apollo finger tells of an unwavering commitment to her own projects and its very length measures how burning is her need to shine through in her career. And it's not just the long finger which emphasises Apollo's influence; look how clear the Apollo line is, neatly placed below the fleshy lower phalange of the finger; and the mount is wide and airy. Having Apollo at such a pitch highlights an appreciation of beauty and everything out of the ordinary. It's a fortunate influence that enhances the rare talents of any individual. All in all, Beryl is dedicated to the artistic and comfortable side of life.

Saturn, being high on the palm, testifies to Beryl's more serious side, and displays a good balance between logic and emotion. But this needs to be watched: too long a Saturn finger can imply depression. I felt instinctively that her Saturn finger was clamouring for attention and it evoked for me a sense of remorse and hanging on to the past that should be controlled. I suspect that she sometimes has to turn in on herself and block other people out of her life.

But without a doubt Jupiter is as powerful as the other two fingers – what's particularly interesting to note is that it's not in the length that it dominates but in the width of the phalanges. This is another driving force putting the needs of self first, and it may make Beryl a little fussy.

All together, then, the three fingers reign over her nature so firmly that Beryl is inevitably directed by her desires. But don't forget that since Apollo is the warm Sun finger its strength means that her need to succeed doesn't initially stop with herself. The influence of tall Apollo ignites internal warmth, generosity and sharing, encouraging expansive ideas and feelings. So it's not all push, push, push on her own behalf!

WAIFS AND STRAYS

Many folk are aware of Beryl's love for her ten stray pussycats, but how many know that her love of animals is powerfully reflected in her hands? Apollo again, together with the thick lower phalanges of the fingers, emphasises the domestic side of the personality and a love of animals that's almost maternal. Her sensitive, touching hands would have a natural flair for nurturing the less fortunate creatures of this world.

MERCURIAL MIND

Despite the dominance of the three other fingers, Mercury's power isn't overshadowed. The finger is a good length so Beryl must have vigorous powers of communication and a certain flair with words. It does seem to shelter beneath Apollo though so this flair of hers will be exercised entirely through the theatrical or any publicly flamboyant sphere. Since the planet Mercury rules the brain, this finger helps make up for any deficiency in Beryl's timid and hesitant head line – but it cannot compensate for it completely (for of course fingers relate to our desires while the lines on the palm actually reflect our true capabilities). You'll have to study this quiet head line deeply it's so faint, which highlights again how ultra-sensitive she is.

FINGERS
Which one wins, Apollo or Saturn? Both fingers are long and emphasise external communication, a mixture of seclusion and extrovert involvement. Flamboyant, outgoing self-expression and the need to be in control of one's own life. Self-preservation is the order of the day. See how much wider the phalanges are on the Jupiter finger, giving it strength despite its relative shortness.

TALENT LINES
Variety is the word here. Many lines over the Mercury mount just above the heart line show she has unlimited resources, she finds new interests all the time and has talents in abundance. They also represent her love of gathering friends, children and animals around her.

MERCURY MOUNT
Vertical markings here run over the matrimonial lines, interfering with partnerships. Marriage/love/personal relationships are thus of lower priority to Beryl than commercial/artistic involvements in life outside the home.

FATE LINE
Runs right up to the Saturn finger, ensuring an active life and career for Beryl into old age.

MERCURY/HEALTH LINE
This fascinating line stems from the Mercury mount to link with the life line, still very much in the area of Moon. Poor health is therefore in evidence, blocking Beryl's path for a while, but this forceful link with the outside communication area means that Beryl can still make the effort to mix. She's no recluse!

LIFE LINE
Tails off three-quarters of the way down the hand, but an inner line takes over as a support. Strength to help Beryl outdo or accept fate!

Beryl Reid

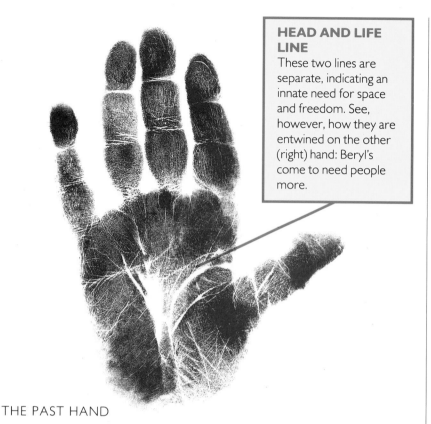

HEAD AND LIFE LINE
These two lines are separate, indicating an innate need for space and freedom. See, however, how they are entwined on the other (right) hand: Beryl's come to need people more.

THE PAST HAND

SLEIGHT OF HEART?

The dainty, rather skittish heart line is very eloquent in this palm. It ends under Saturn, showing how she tends to be defensive; I wouldn't say selfish but self-protective. You can see how feathery and patchy this line is; it seemed rather cheeky and flirtatious to me. These qualities urge Beryl to act on impulse and indulge her whims! The slightness of the line means that her affections may not be long-lasting; sustaining her emotional obligations would probably be a bit too much for this free-thinking individual.

I'd say that fate had little to do with the first part of Beryl's life, taking second place to her own initiative and sheer will, for the fate line only rises in the centre palm. It breaks away from the Mercury/Health line about the late 30s: maybe a period of ill health or emotional trauma then made her more willing to listen to its promptings? Its influence is therefore stronger as maturity sets in. The line runs right up to the base of the Saturn finger, full of energy far into the future, so an active lifestyle in her career or otherwise is planned for Beryl right into old age (providing nothing gets in the way).

I found these hands full of spiritual knowledge, but felt that she has not finished with her journeys on earth – she'll be back! For the call of her spiritual destiny is somewhat hazy – perhaps she prefers to pay more attention to her earthbound path? Only time will let her see things with clearer eyes as regards spiritual duties.

She tends to magnify everything out of proportion and is prone to rapid changes of mind, which must have made her intellectual development rather erratic; she'll have found it hard to concentrate. There are numerous dots and patches covering the palm emphasising how overreacting to circumstances may have marred her progress and personal friendships. The weakness of the head line does suggest an outspoken disposition, so she'll either win friends – or lose them!

HAND TO HAND

On the right hand, Beryl's active growing hand (main picture), the head and life lines are entwined, telling how she now needs others and values their companionship. This is not so on the left hand where they are separate: her innate personality can cope with independence, and indeed needs space and freedom. Another change is the fullness and roundness of the right palm (much larger than the tiny left one) which shows how she has reached a point where she feels almost totally fulfilled by life but it still exudes a great deal of sensitivity. There are lines running from the Moon mount into Venus showing how she constantly needs to be active; because she's not too well at the moment, and is convalescing after hospital treatment, this must be sheer torment – her personality craves contact but the physical problems must frustrate her. Her life line on the right hand seems to accept this – it's unbroken – so she's making the best of the present situation. It splits into two lines in the mid 40s, a time when she must have settled for a quieter phase, and since then she's appreciated home comforts more. Of the two lines one turns into the Venus mount, the other travels towards Moon, indicating that she desires the contrast of two lifestyles continually, one home-based and one involved with the public.

DEREK GRIFFITHS

P·R·O·F·I·L·E

Actor, mime artist, musician, children's TV presenter

Date of Birth: 15 July 1946

Sun Sign: CANCER

Element: Water

Ruling Planet: Moon

A perfect example of an organiser extraordinaire! Derek's a larger-than-life character, versatile and extremely methodical, all of which is there to be seen in the overall shape of his hands and in the orderly pattern around the thumbs. He's a good time-keeper, with an inner clock that's utterly reliable. And he's brimful with energy – there are no signs of physical fatigue in his hands.

HEY LOOK, IT'S ME!

Derek's palms are loud and simply crying out to be noticed – look at the way Apollo clings to Saturn in the right palm. This also shows that he values others and their opinions, and if they praise and reward him it will spur him on to new heights. He's adventurous and carefree and adaptable, all witnessed by the suppleness of the hands and the easy balance of lines on the palm. He can survive the most turbulent of times with panache. I felt a sense of tidiness in him which encourages people to rely on Derek and he will always respond, for he is conscious of his obligations towards others no less than towards himself. He won't let anyone down, nor will he divert one inch from his set goals.

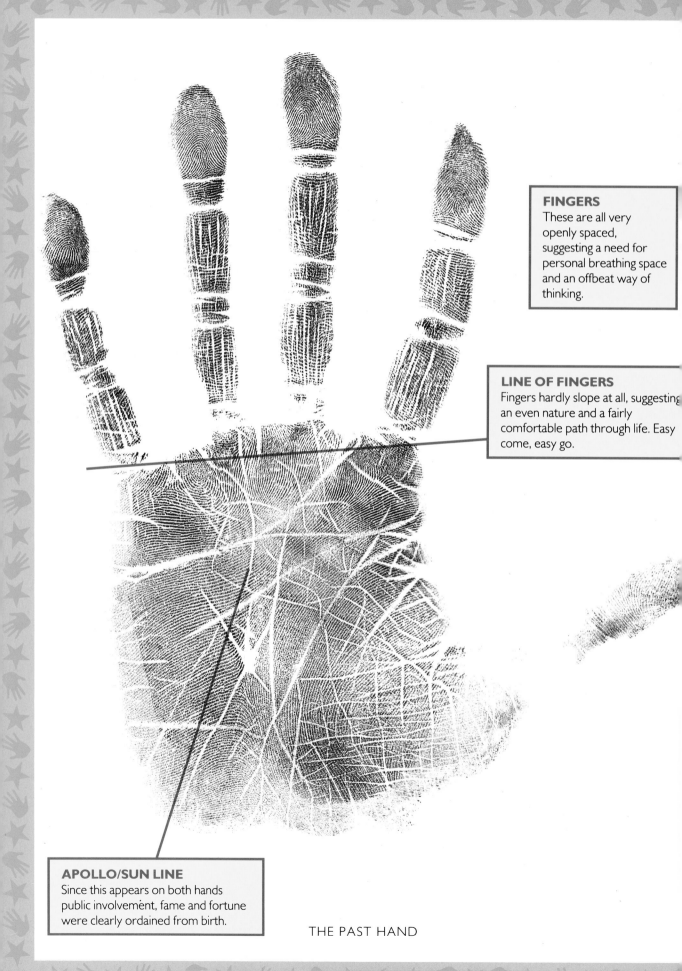

FINGERS
These are all very openly spaced, suggesting a need for personal breathing space and an offbeat way of thinking.

LINE OF FINGERS
Fingers hardly slope at all, suggesting an even nature and a fairly comfortable path through life. Easy come, easy go.

APOLLO/SUN LINE
Since this appears on both hands public involvement, fame and fortune were clearly ordained from birth.

THE PAST HAND

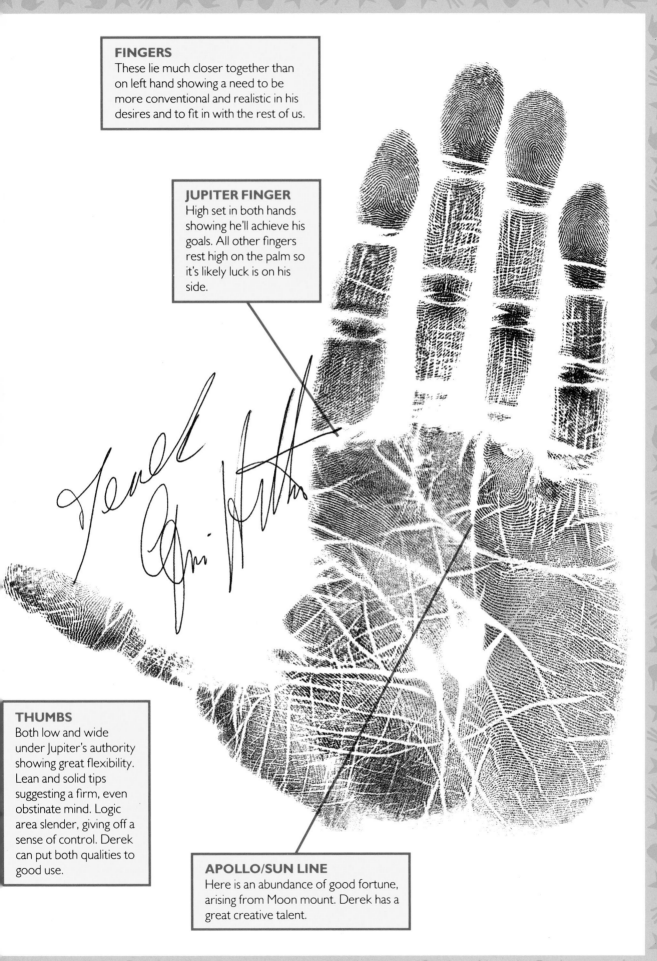

FINGERS
These lie much closer together than on left hand showing a need to be more conventional and realistic in his desires and to fit in with the rest of us.

JUPITER FINGER
High set in both hands showing he'll achieve his goals. All other fingers rest high on the palm so it's likely luck is on his side.

THUMBS
Both low and wide under Jupiter's authority showing great flexibility. Lean and solid tips suggesting a firm, even obstinate mind. Logic area slender, giving off a sense of control. Derek can put both qualities to good use.

APOLLO/SUN LINE
Here is an abundance of good fortune, arising from Moon mount. Derek has a great creative talent.

STRENGTH AND SADNESS

The surface of the skin is tough, reflecting Derek's resilience. Nothing gets at him! This very solidity makes him self-disciplined but sometimes too hard on himself. The palms lie quite flat except for a little hollow in the centre revealing a disappointment, or an air of unfulfilment. Perhaps he's not found 'true love' or not completely satisfied himself at work? Whichever, this hollow has yet to be filled. Apart from this, Derek's hands look 'straight' and clear, suggesting constant achievement. Perhaps this feeling that there's something missing from his life stems from the fact he has not had to strive unduly for what he's achieved?

MIND GAMES

Derek's head line is as energetic as the man himself, sloping down into the Moon area and almost linking up with the travel lines there – but this means that he can't slow his brain down enough to stop thoughts churning round and round in his mind. The length of this swooping head line emphasises a prolific imagination and ingenuity far above the norm. I imagine his sprightly mentality is inherited.

O LUCKY MAN . . .

These are lucky palms. Not that Derek has not had to work hard for his living, but things do seem to fall into place for him, as betrayed by the even, flat line made by the finger bases. This also conveys his calm temper and relaxed nature. Every mark is clear cut in the hand, leaving no muddled thoughts, banishing any feelings of remorse. There are two powerful pointers toward success: the Apollo line and the way it connects with the fate line. Such lines can bestow riches beyond one's wildest dreams and since Derek's are developed beneath the Apollo

and Saturn fingers these riches will relate to his inner potential as well as material things. So he'll profit from his talent for self-expression by succeeding in his chosen artistic sphere and fulfilling all his hopes and dreams – some time. A rare blessing!

Look at the wide-open fingers on the left hand. This of course shows a free spirit – add the laid-back thumb and it's easy to see that Derek is liberated, radiating a certain sexual charisma. There's lots of energy in this area of his life – he really launches himself into lovemaking. The unconventionality and alert, spontaneous approach to life make me feel that he's not only confident but a very versatile and

adventurous lover. The mischievous streak running through the loose thumbs only reiterates this. So – lucky the partner that can catch him – and keep him. And to cap it all, the heart line is strong and healthy revealing a sense of purpose in this area!

However, the finger spacing could not be more different on the right hand – airy and uncluttered has given way to close-knit with the leading finger leaning inward to the ruling Saturn digit. This stimulates his self-assertiveness and will bind people to him. People have always been attracted by his easy-going nature in the past, but even more now as Derek has come to need their comradeship. He needs to fit into society. He needs to be close to the world. O lucky world!

DOROTHY TUTIN

·P·R·O·F·I·L·E·

Actress

Date of Birth: 8 April 1930

Sun Sign: ARIES

Element: Fire

Ruling Planet: Mars

What fascinating, finely-etched, dainty hands! Tiny palms like these often hold vast reserves of courage and Dorothy's are no exception. Behind the outer façade there's a perseverance that shines through the wide-open lines and fingers which can balance desires and action without any problem at all.

FRAGILE FLIGHTS OF FANCY
Dorothy's palms are very active in the area of Neptune which rules the imagination. Its influence is so strong here that her capacity for fantasy could well override reality with spine-tingling and intriguing possibilities. Artistic and cultural pursuits inspire her, and her palms look very youthful. Her

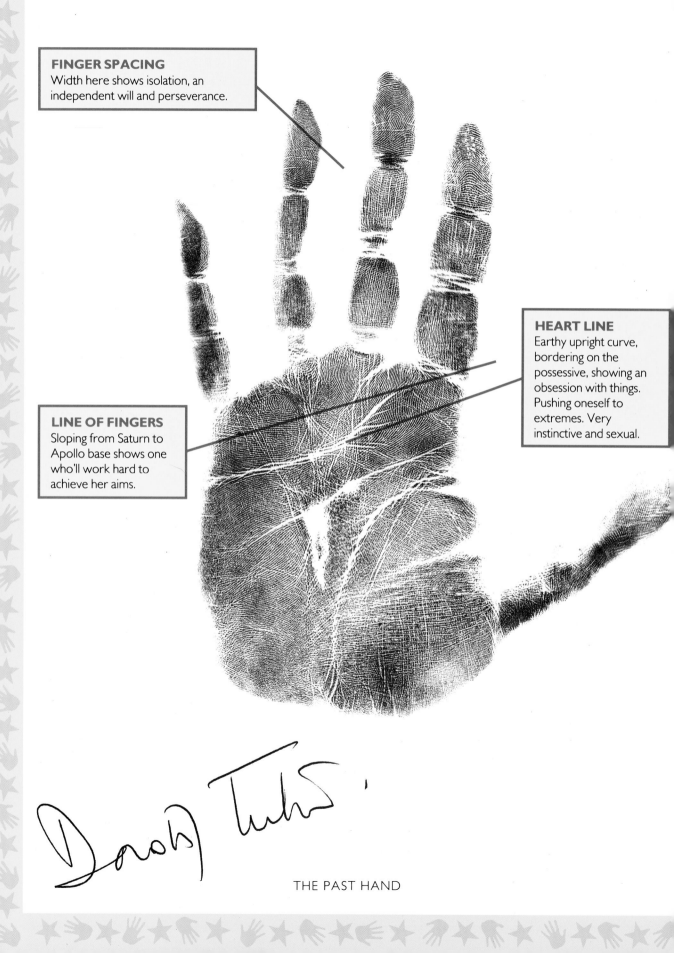

FINGER SPACING
Width here shows isolation, an independent will and perseverance.

LINE OF FINGERS
Sloping from Saturn to Apollo base shows one who'll work hard to achieve her aims.

HEART LINE
Earthy upright curve, bordering on the possessive, showing an obsession with things. Pushing oneself to extremes. Very instinctive and sexual.

THE PAST HAND

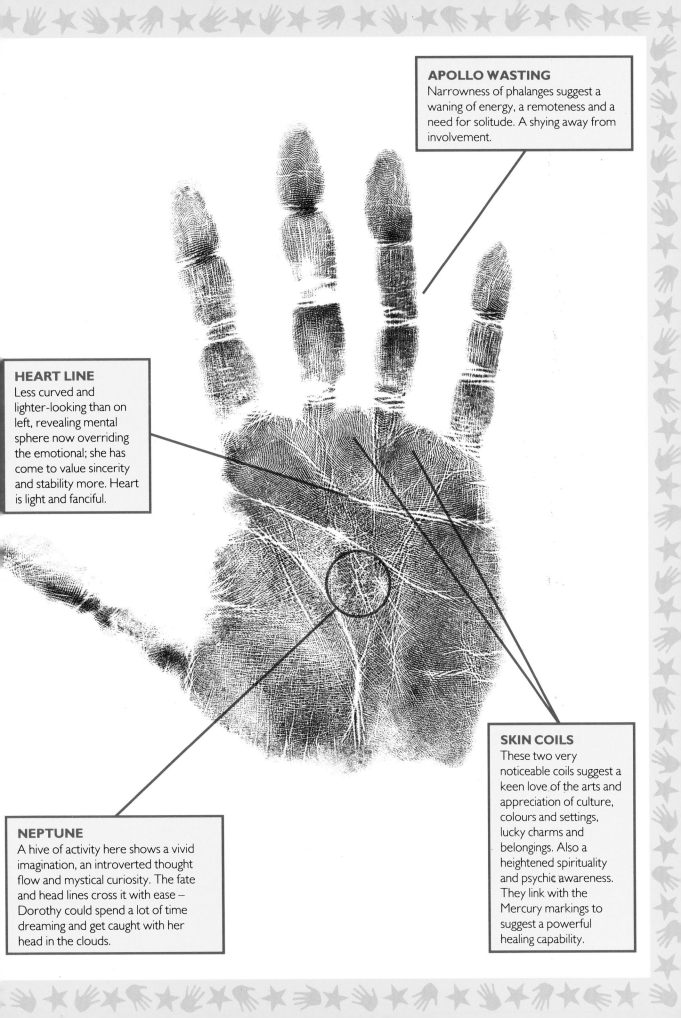

APOLLO WASTING
Narrowness of phalanges suggest a waning of energy, a remoteness and a need for solitude. A shying away from involvement.

HEART LINE
Less curved and lighter-looking than on left, revealing mental sphere now overriding the emotional; she has come to value sincerity and stability more. Heart is light and fanciful.

SKIN COILS
These two very noticeable coils suggest a keen love of the arts and appreciation of culture, colours and settings, lucky charms and belongings. Also a heightened spirituality and psychic awareness. They link with the Mercury markings to suggest a powerful healing capability.

NEPTUNE
A hive of activity here shows a vivid imagination, an introverted thought flow and mystical curiosity. The fate and head lines cross it with ease – Dorothy could spend a lot of time dreaming and get caught with her head in the clouds.

head line is deep-seated, inspiring an almost poetic contrast between the spiritual and analytical in her thinking. She has an intellectual and aware mind.

Both palms are obviously delicate, a slightness that gives off a fragile charisma but suggests that she finds rudeness and criticism hard to bear. The left hand is slightly smaller than the right, so her basic nature is introverted (but not without confidence) while the more rounded right shows that the soul has quietly matured and learnt over the years – and that strength and dedication have been with her always. There's little difference in the lines and finger spacing between the two hands but the smaller left hand certainly reveals a delicate child who may have had a restricted upbringing. Nowadays she has an assertiveness that others may underestimate but mostly she lives in her Neptune-inspired dream world where she can devote her energy to Art, living for each day at a time.

ALL WORK AND NO PLAY?
Where the bases of the fingers link into the palms it's interesting to note the slope from Saturn (left hand) to Mercury, which suggests a hard worker, a dedicated stickler. She deserves the just rewards of her endurance. While she may sometimes want to reject the world, her staying power to battle on never falters. She's a sympathetic character, a woman of precision whose self-sufficiency will always allow her vibrant imagination to come into play.

POSSESSIONS AND OBSESSIONS
The Saturn mount is placed low and the fingertip turns slightly, making Dorothy rather vulnerable to melancholy and

reluctant to close the book on past chapters of her life. Another tell-tale sign is the delicate, tattered life line on the left hand. It can't take disturbances. And then there's the skin coils below the finger of art, culture, hobbies and creativity – Apollo – denoting a heightened sensitivity. These influences lean towards belongings as does the far-reaching heart line which wants to collect and hoard things, and the podgy Jupiter finger which wants to control possessions and people. Here's a keen love of the unusual, a certain superstitiousness and an affinity for lucky charms. Mother Earth is influencing her to nurture and store.

RUN WILD AND FREE
Dorothy has a marvellous head line for promoting writing skills – stories, poetry and memoirs. It's racing across the hand almost blending with the travel area where thoughts flower rapidly. Abundant imagination and artistic expression stems from the eager mind, but sadly the head line is rather weak, showing a delicate mental constitution and an inner restlessness where the personality flits like a butterfly from one thing to another. Yet though she may lose her way all too frequently the depths of her nature can revive optimism and mental vigour.

A SPICE TO LIFE
The left heart line (past hand) curves up markedly, touching Jupiter mount and revealing clinging emotion and a need for attention and attachments. This is an instinctive heart line, so sexual encounters would be judged on the intuitive level. There's less of a curve to the right heart line so nowadays reason and practical judgement are more in evidence, and sexual satisfaction is found through a more direct approach. She's an

intense, passionate woman – see the long, low-set thumbs and spontaneous openness of the lines and fingers. She can understand and care for others warmly, but the appetite for career has overtaken that for love. The Sun line smooths over a split in the heart and would take command over any emotional problems, and as it reaches down towards the head line it must encourage her artistic success and mental inspiration as well as wealth and recognition. She's a good communicator, truly empathetic towards others. Her receptive mind soaks up knowledge like a sponge.

I intuitively felt that Dorothy is a rather lonely individual with deep-seated wounds that remain open, making her tread warily through new experiences and keeping her rather distant. The Apollo fingers look wasted and tired, which shows a lethargic indifference towards relationships. The separation of Apollo and Saturn suggest she'll make it through life on her own. A declaration of independence to be reckoned with!

BILL TREACHER

·P·R·O·F·I·L·E·

Actor, 'Arthur' in *EastEnders*

Date of Birth: Not given

Sun Sign: GEMINI

Element: Air

Ruling Planet: Mercury

The tough skin on Bill's hands makes them feel as solid as they look – but there is a delicate shadow that I sensed about them. They were fleshy and enormously energetic, the hands of a man eager to please and take up challenges. He's a caring, attentive, compassionate man who identifies with others, so he'd never neglect them in his active search to fulfil his ambitions. And in that search he's aware of his limitations – he knows that if other people take over he'll rebel and become rather disorganised as a result. The squareness of his palms shows he can abide by a certain amount of law and order, but he cannot tolerate too much routine. He needs new sensations to excite him and satisfy his searching curiosity, and to be free to move on as and when he wishes – particularly since he is an Air person who needs space in which to stretch and into which to expel his frustrations.

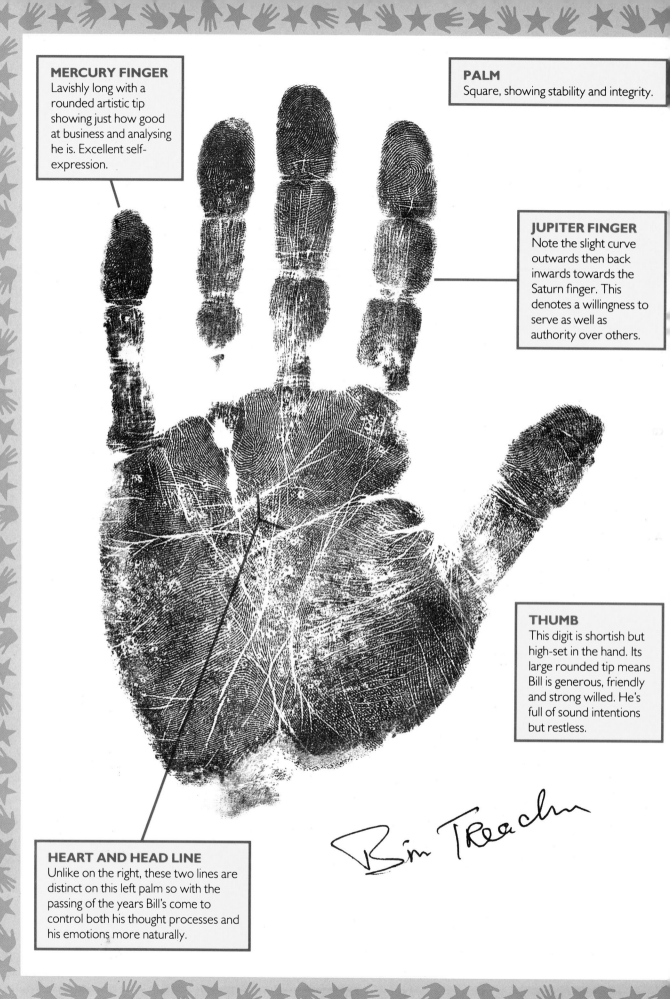

MERCURY FINGER
Lavishly long with a rounded artistic tip showing just how good at business and analysing he is. Excellent self-expression.

PALM
Square, showing stability and integrity.

JUPITER FINGER
Note the slight curve outwards then back inwards towards the Saturn finger. This denotes a willingness to serve as well as authority over others.

THUMB
This digit is shortish but high-set in the hand. Its large rounded tip means Bill is generous, friendly and strong willed. He's full of sound intentions but restless.

HEART AND HEAD LINE
Unlike on the right, these two lines are distinct on this left palm so with the passing of the years Bill's come to control both his thought processes and his emotions more naturally.

Bill Treacher

FAMILY TIES

Bill comes from a supportive and caring family background, a fact attested to by the deliberate family and social ties that cross Mount Venus so impressively. And if he didn't come from a large family, certainly the home base involves him above all else. On his right hand – the past, for Bill is left-handed – the head and heart lines entwine in an unusual way which must mean life has been awkward for him in the past. He must have been clumsy in his affections, either seeing things too simplistically or reading too much into them, because he is governed entirely by his instincts. This conflict has resolved itself with the passing of the years for these energies no longer confuse in the left palm. So the intellect is sharper and capable of understanding things quite naturally. He can distinguish his feelings easily and his thought processes have lost their timidity. He's definitely in control.

A ROUGH RIDE

When I read Bill's hands they both looked patchy and irritable, indicating low health – and not just in the physical sense but in the psychological too. The erratic and isolated white patches in the prints confirm an internal disorder that's making him lethargic and disinterested in life at the moment. Bill told me he's had a skin problem recently which may account for the roughness and the slightly white appearance, but it does not explain the fundamentally hazy look which highlights a delicate constitution just now. These markings aren't located in any one area, which suggests an overall imbalance. Perhaps he's carrying a heavy personal burden? The pitted, messy look to the life line and mount Venus reiterates the health problem but one which is probably affecting his emotions more than his physical well-being. Something

needs to be sorted out – and soon – to restore the missing gaiety and sparkle to Bill's normally effervescent nature. He's tired and seeking a solution – look at the frayed life line mourning the loss of happier days. There's particular lack of energy in the decade between 38 and 48, showing nervous stress and general depression. Rest is in order then more than at any other time. But in his 40s to 50s Bill will be able to throw off some restriction of the past and revitalise himself because there's a major breakthrough on the life line when he'll finally be free to test new, refreshing waters.

HARMONY AND HIGH STANDARDS

There's a formidable balance in the finger spacing and line separation revealing how little conflict there is within Bill's fundamental personality. Here's a man outwardly very confident, with enough enthusiasm to carry him over the most turbulent of waves. Yet the slight knitting of head and life lines early in life reminds us that he does need loved ones around him and occasionally he relies on their support. Bill is certainly friendly, but values a few selected friends most and has little or no time for

hangers-on or greedy, stupid people. He values integrity and fairness in everyone – denoted by the high set and well-shaped thumb. His Jupiter finger sways slightly outward and then defers respectfully to its elder brother Saturn, a curve that wants to relate to and serve others while being in command. Jupiter is also the finger of perfection – Bill's a provider and a striver, seeking to accomplish goals in his own way, following his own rules. Look back at the versatile, self-reliant thumbs with their heavy tips reflecting his strength of mind and purpose.

Bill is trebly ruled by Mercury the communicator – it's his ruling planet, his Mercury fingers are very tall and the mount is thickly covered with lines. So it's no wonder we have an artistic communicator, an analyser, an intelligent businessman, a master of words. His powers of self-expression are so emphasised that I think he could just as easily have been a counsellor, teacher or lawyer as an actor. Perhaps he ought to try his hand at producing? Certainly if you gave him a soap box he'd be in his element!

THE PAST HAND

HEART AND HEAD LINE
The way these lines link up confuse Bill and aggravate inner doubts and restrictions. Luckily only seen on past hand.

JUNE BROWN

·P·R·O·F·I·L·E·

Actress, 'Dot Cotton' in *EastEnders*

Date of Birth: 16 February

Sun Sign: AQUARIUS

Element: Air

Ruling Planet: Uranus/Saturn

What is immediately striking about June's palms are their length and multitude of lines. This means that outside stimulation will always impel June into action. I found a logical and direct approach to life here and no matter how much the length of the palms tries to promote the imaginative side of her nature, the reasonable and stable elements take priority. The constant line activity here, especially on the Moon and Venus mounts, reveal fantasy and dreams, only to be diffused by the sharp mental process as the head line moves steadily across the palms. The breadth of the palms reiterates this secure focus and highlights her common sense.

Her sensible attitude doesn't imply coldness, though; I found each phalange endearing and fertile, and a generous lean to the hands revealed warmth. This is particularly noticeable on the Mercury mount with its plentiful vertical markings that encourage June's willing, caring personality. The fingers are generally erect and firm (she likes to find straightness and fairness in the people around her) but the Saturn finger on the left hand does lean towards Apollo, and the Sun finger returns the compliment. This shows that June will always be happy both alone or in company; that she responds tenderly to people and their creative projects. But on the other side of the coin are the feelings of melancholy that she can't escape, reflected in Saturn's warp. This isn't so pronounced in the right hand – there the Apollo finger brings out just the opposite. This makes me feel that June tends to wait for situations to arise nowadays rather than consciously pushing them along. The initiative's still there, but a little laziness means she has to push herself hard to find motivation. Both Jupiter fingers suggest that she has a dominating inner strength; link this with the healthy will power and you have some rather dictatorial tendencies . . .

PSYCHIC POWER

June's dreamy thought flow puts up a barrier between herself and outsiders that hides the serious layer from whence her talent springs. Her head line is quite strong, sloping toward the edge of the Moon mount, and has a great capacity for learning. But this capacity is not confined to the here and now, she is acutely aware of spiritual and psychic energies, and her soul has been learning esoterically for so long that it is now fully developed. June is a 'student of life', and busy lines all over the hands tell

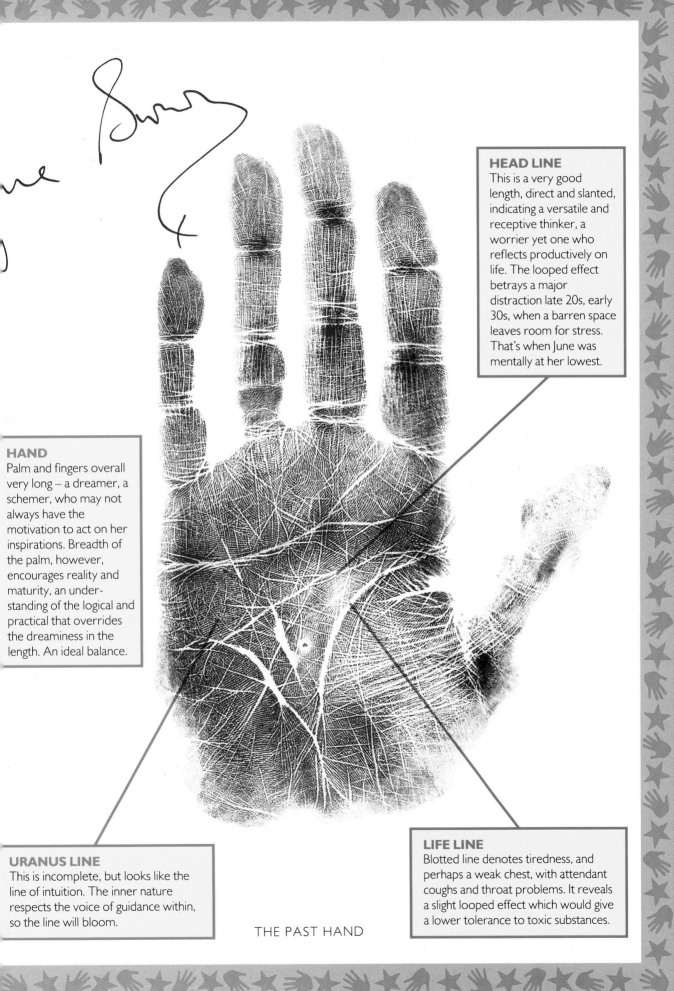

HEAD LINE
This is a very good length, direct and slanted, indicating a versatile and receptive thinker, a worrier yet one who reflects productively on life. The looped effect betrays a major distraction late 20s, early 30s, when a barren space leaves room for stress. That's when June was mentally at her lowest.

HAND
Palm and fingers overall very long – a dreamer, a schemer, who may not always have the motivation to act on her inspirations. Breadth of the palm, however, encourages reality and maturity, an under-standing of the logical and practical that overrides the dreaminess in the length. An ideal balance.

URANUS LINE
This is incomplete, but looks like the line of intuition. The inner nature respects the voice of guidance within, so the line will bloom.

LIFE LINE
Blotted line denotes tiredness, and perhaps a weak chest, with attendant coughs and throat problems. It reveals a slight looped effect which would give a lower tolerance to toxic substances.

THE PAST HAND

of many spiritual rebirths. She may well be aware of the paths she trod in previous incarnations, and I sense that she is on one of her final Karmic paths. I found what is probably a line of Uranus penetrating the outer edge of the Moon mount. If this is indeed a true shadow of Uranus it confirms June's psychic ability and intuition. She has another highly developed capacity – to serve others. If she were not an actress a counselling or healing profession would have suited her, for a healing power is reflected in the deeply-etched heart line and the lines running over mount Mercury.

BRIGHT LIGHTS BECKONING

What about June's career? This looks very healthy; career implications are seen in the fate line which extends way up into the crevice of the Saturn fingers, meaning that, God willing, she can go on working into old age. As one door closes another will open, no fading into obscurity for June: there's great activity in both the past and the future. That she's in the public eye is confirmed by the fate lines stemming from the Moon area, but it must be said that their broken and scattered effect fill June's career with uncertain episodes. Compare this with the life line; it's also fairly energetic but with clearly unfavourable periods at the outset. From the age of 40 fortunate signs make June more secure, but not for long, sadly; the mid to late 40s are unsettled (small dots blur inside the life line halfway down). Improvement won't come till the early 50s, and between 50 and 53 she will radically break away from her old lifestyle – and then again at 60. A move may help for a short while but won't be the long-term answer.

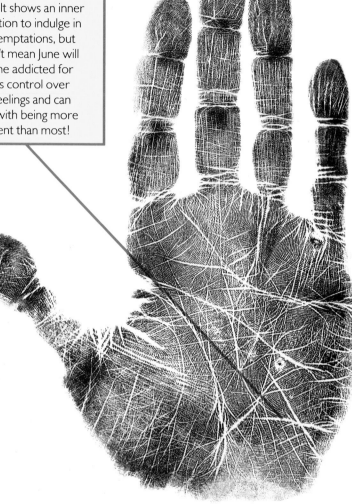

VIA LASCIVA
Indicating a strong love of rich food, drink, toxic substances and everything that depletes goodness from the body! It shows an inner inclination to indulge in such temptations, but doesn't mean June will become addicted for she has control over such feelings and can cope with being more indulgent than most!

Firmness and sharpness in these hands shouldn't obscure the sensitivity of the sunny heart line, the healing marks and the outgoing mount Venus that rule in the final analysis. Emotions are deeply rooted but unfortunately diffuse – fluctuations of the heart line with its loops and sketchy patches expose discontent. Relationships along the way have not been all that they should. The heart line splits just below the Apollo mount so June must have severed her ties with someone in her late 20s, leaving herself prone to restlessness. Affection and companionship come and go in short spells for her emotions are spontaneous but not necessarily long lasting – this means June needs tolerance and flexibility to endure personal ups and downs. And indeed she has plenty of stamina to overcome life's trials and tribulations for confidence and personal freedom are inbred in the hand. It matters little to June where she belongs, just as long as she *can*!

MATTHEW KELLY

·P·R·O·F·I·L·E·

Actor, comedian

Date of Birth: 9 May 1950

Sun Sign: TAURUS

Element: Earth

Ruling Planet: Venus

Just one glance at these enormous hands and you know that Matthew is as vibrant and extrovert as his public image. The skin is remarkably sensitive, confirming what we all knew, he's a big softie at heart! He's a nostalgic character – look how the left Saturn fingertip turns over towards Apollo – memories die hard. But he's generally adaptable (very supple hands) and can make his home anywhere. Material security is important (the second phalanges of each finger are very solid looking) but that doesn't stop him testing himself with new ventures and leaving behind the safety of the familiar. His sensitivity to people and life helps keep his feet on the ground.

These palms have an overall air of physical well-being, a physicality that extends into his love of fresh air and nature. But this co-exists with his love of artistic and cultural things revealed in the well-proportioned lower phalanges and broad, outgoing lower palm. His sharp mind is reflected in the roomy uncluttered nature of his hands and the responsiveness of the skin texture highlights his awareness of the world around him.

A FREE SPIRIT

The large and vibrant Venus area reveals both generosity and great passion. Matthew doesn't seem to have any inhibitions when it comes to sexuality, taking into account the openness of the palm, fingers and thumbs as well as the rounded Venus mount. He's quick to respond and likes everything clear-cut and tidy, then collects himself rapidly after the excitement. For there is a little aloofness in the Saturn area which probably makes him dislike the thought of actually belonging to any one person. His heart line is rather looped, making it unlikely he'd remain constant within a relationship. The whole hands throw off challenge and change – and the heart line is just the same. Always looking for that new experience . . .

FROM PAST TO PRESENT

The life line, arched toward the centre palm, is pushing him into contact with other people – his excitement in travel and fresh experiences overcomes the serious shaping of the Saturn fingers which move him in the opposite direction. His temperament calls for a balance of stillness and noise around him.

The influence of the powerful Saturn finger should never be ignored. It's the leader of the palm, and as Matthew's leans away from Jupiter at the tip it suggests the moroseness, love of solitude and clinging to the past I've already mentioned. It could even lead him into depression but for the controlling effect of the solid, normal-length head line. Things have improved because the Saturn finger on the current (right) hand is a better shape. I reckon Matthew's come to terms with this moodier side to his character; in fact, he's loosened up generally – the Jupiter/Saturn spacing in the past shows how guarded Matthew could be, but it's freer now. The changes in finger spacing (especially between Apollo/Saturn and Jupiter/Saturn), the easier looking head line and the more natural separation of head and life line show that Matthew has far better judgement and powers of reason these days. His melancholy has faded into memory.

Similarly, there is a firmer sense of direction in the fate line. It is very uncontrolled in the past (left) hand and Matthew must have had a rather turbulent ride earlier in life. Happily it's much smoother in the right hand which means he's come to a better understanding of himself and his vocation. The fate line is interrupted at around the ages 38, 41, 45, 49 to early 50s. The disturbance at 37 to 38 shows a draining of emotions: perhaps the end of a friendship? The others refer to times when Matthew will be forced to accept new patterns in his life and adjust to a new routine – possibly taxing but often rewarding phases of his life. In fact, mid life (i.e. 41) heralds a very happy time – either through the discovery of a hidden talent or a new relationship.

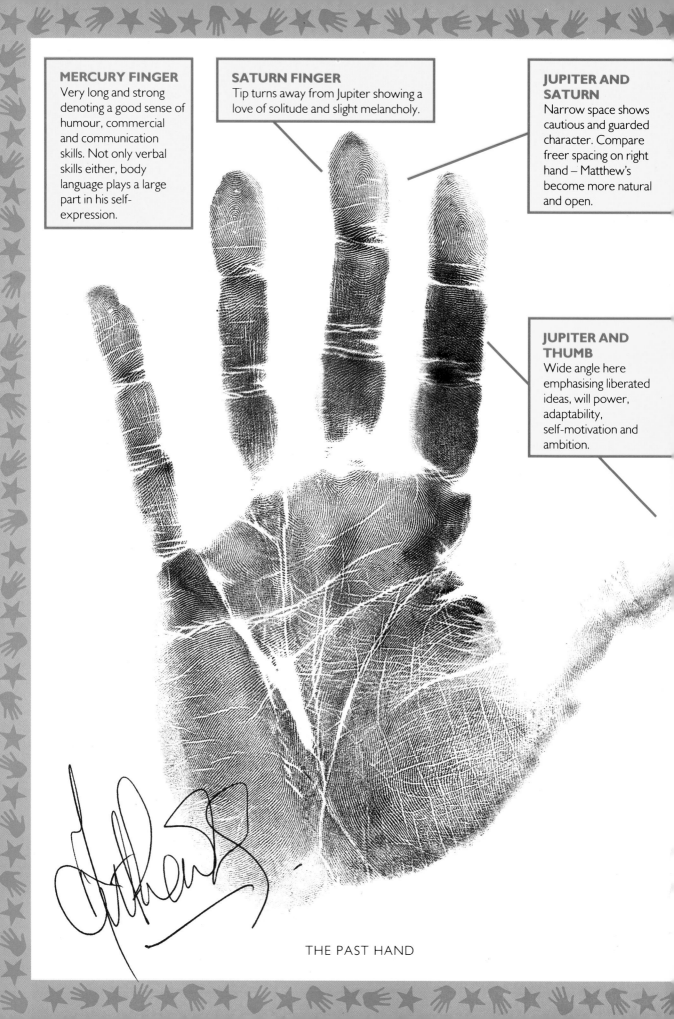

MERCURY FINGER
Very long and strong denoting a good sense of humour, commercial and communication skills. Not only verbal skills either, body language plays a large part in his self-expression.

SATURN FINGER
Tip turns away from Jupiter showing a love of solitude and slight melancholy.

JUPITER AND SATURN
Narrow space shows cautious and guarded character. Compare freer spacing on right hand – Matthew's become more natural and open.

JUPITER AND THUMB
Wide angle here emphasising liberated ideas, will power, adaptability, self-motivation and ambition.

THE PAST HAND

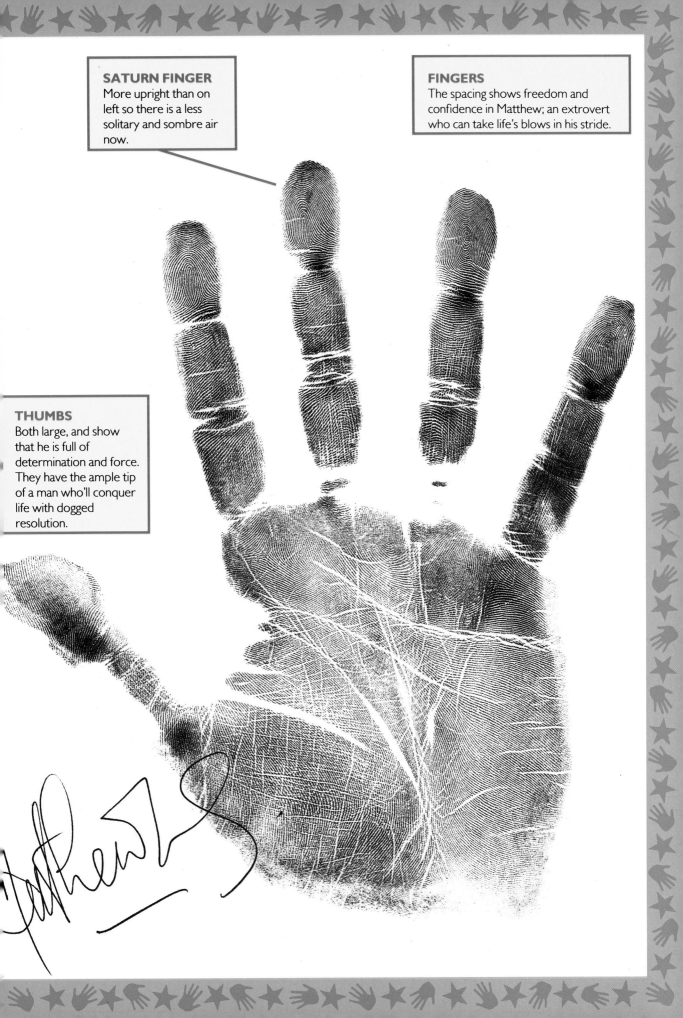

SATURN FINGER
More upright than on left so there is a less solitary and sombre air now.

FINGERS
The spacing shows freedom and confidence in Matthew; an extrovert who can take life's blows in his stride.

THUMBS
Both large, and show that he is full of determination and force. They have the ample tip of a man who'll conquer life with dogged resolution.

SU POLLARD

·P·R·O·F·I·L·E·

Actress, star of *Hi-De-Hi!*

Date of Birth: 7 November 1949
Sun Sign: SCORPIO
Element: Water
Ruling Planet: Pluto/Mars

It comes as no surprise to find effervescence in Su's palms! You can see the clear spacing between all the fingers and the wide-angled thumbs, and the sweeping lines, betraying a go-getting spirit. The palms look fleshy and energetic, particularly around the base of the Jupiter fingers, which shows tremendous physical energy. They're thick too, implying aggression of spirit as well as of body. Su's versatility and range of talents are reflected in the outer curve of the palm.

BLESSED WITH ZEST

Su is left-handed so that's her progressive hand. And it reveals steadfastness, liveliness and an abundance of vitality. Here's a warrior on the battlefield of life – and one on the winning side. Her knuckles are firm and well marked; if you link this with the seriousness of Saturn and the length of the head lines you can see that she's both sensible and alert. The thumbs, although placed low on the hand, are short and sharp and the lower phalanges (indicating reasoning powers) are stronger than the area of will and obstinacy. Yet, although she does take the time to ponder the practicalities, I found an air of movement in the palms that shows she also likes to follow her impulses. As for her uniquely extrovert fashion sense (and her *remarkable* powers of self-expression!) these are sparked off by the long Apollo finger and Mercury's powerful influence.

The Apollo finger really stands out as its tip climbs steadily towards Saturn, and it's here her work in the theatre is reflected, showing how she needs to display her artistic talents to an audience. Since Apollo points to power and attractiveness in relation to hobbies, business and people it's calling Su to the forefront, encouraging all the adaptability and energy that she brings to her performances.

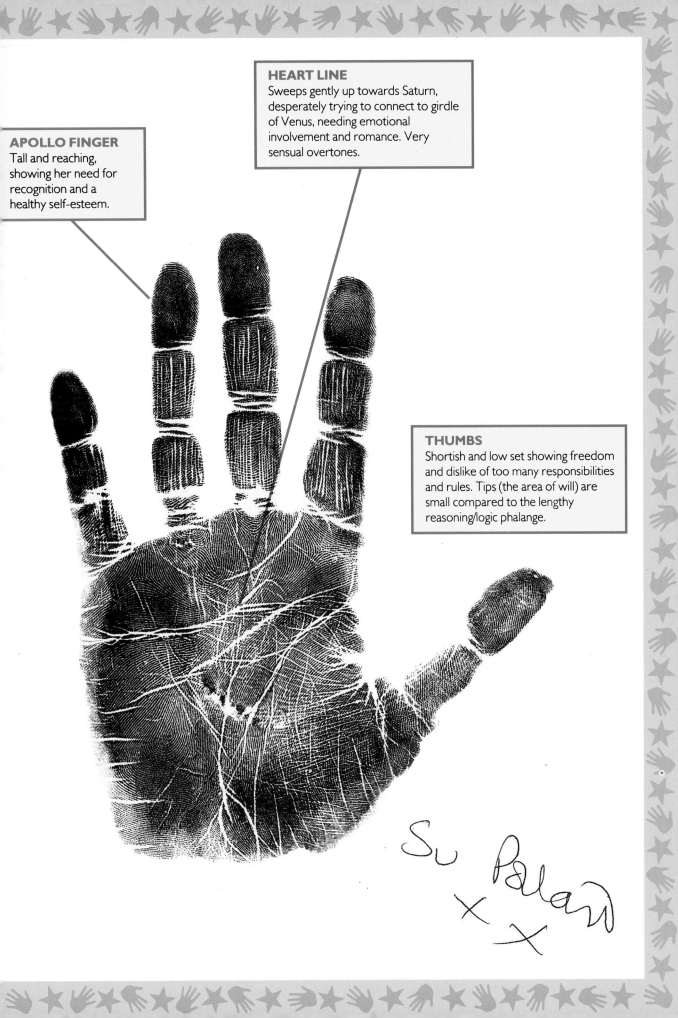

APOLLO FINGER
Tall and reaching, showing her need for recognition and a healthy self-esteem.

HEART LINE
Sweeps gently up towards Saturn, desperately trying to connect to girdle of Venus, needing emotional involvement and romance. Very sensual overtones.

THUMBS
Shortish and low set showing freedom and dislike of too many responsibilities and rules. Tips (the area of will) are small compared to the lengthy reasoning/logic phalange.

Su Pollard
x x

A COOL HEAD

You can also spot impulsiveness and gregariousness in the clear spacing between the head and life lines – she doesn't often tone down her loud, colourful behaviour! But look at the head line driving purposefully across the centre of the palms: this calms her down, showing that she can philosophise (remember the thumbs!) In fact the head line almost runs off the palm altogether, emphasising the length of time she devotes to thought and issues beyond the strictly personal. This also betrays high intelligence and a good memory. Although the energies run quickly and freely through these palms she can balance reality and desires, never losing sight of the practical.

HEAD V. HEART

Looking at the heart line on both palms clearly demonstrates the difference between past and present. In the right (past) hand it's low-set, straight and short, ending under Saturn, which shows her to be ruled basically by her head not her emotions. But on the left (current) palm it's fuller and warmer, high in the hand and sweeping up to join the middle of the girdle of Venus. This shows how Su has mellowed: the old heart line (in the past hand) curves down towards the head line and has a devil of a time untying itself from the head forces which dominate – logical, cautious and challenging. But the new line on the left hand has a gentle upward curve which encourages her femininity and leaves logic

behind; Su's grown more instinctive and responsive with time. But although she's more romantic these days, the heart line hasn't let go of the head altogether (see the two lines breaking off downward to connect with the head line) reminding us how she can be single-minded, and still look after number one. This fork implies a good balance between will and emotion.

Su is physically very demonstrative. She would never hesitate to show her affection through touching someone she loves. But her reaction to others depends on her frame of mind at any given moment: she can adjust to someone's needs instantaneously if so moved and when inspired she'd light up like a colourful beacon. Off on a new adventure! But if there is any hint of a communication barrier she can switch off just as easily. The low, broken, short head line in the right hand bears this out. There is a half semi-circle of Venus which mirrors her sensitive and romantic side. As it's only half formed, though, you can assume that in the final analysis Su's ruled by her head rather than her heart. If you study the palms you can see how her heart line runs clearly in two parallel markings, which shows she needs to fulfil her emotions in all sorts of diverse ways, almost leading a double life to keep pace with her emotional needs. This double composition eases up around the age of 40 to 42 revealing that a more settled and placid picture is imminent.

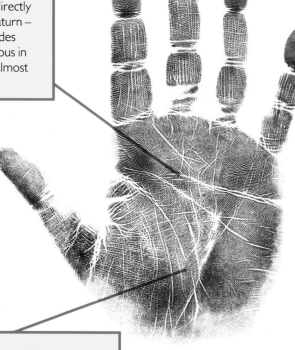

HEART LINE
Low and straight, stopping short directly below mount Saturn – emotional attitudes were more serious in the past. Head almost ruling here.

LIFE LINE
A serious separation of the life line at the age of 42, terminating a pathway in Su's life. Fate's interference will redirect her – see the fate line leading off towards the Saturn mount.

THE PAST HAND

squareness shows her reliability, and the rounded edges to the palms her love of involvement with people and her outgoing worldly character. Then there is the tall Apollo finger showing how ambitious she is. Finally the head line: although it's wavy it strives to hold itself high in the hand, helping her to push on through life. Barbara won't be beaten, no matter what.

THE SUNNY SIDE OF THE STREET?

Barbara is ruled by the Sun so you'd expect a highly developed ego – and indeed you can see this in the palm. Apollo is nearly as tall as Saturn, so, while not actually selfish, self is important to Barbara, and her individuality and personal magnetism dominate, just as the Apollo finger dominates the others. She needs to stand out, unique; no melting into the crowd for her! In fact she may go to extremes, and her tastes aren't always conventional – the fingers are too fleshy to be totally refined. Moreover, she could well end up taking risks, for instincts and impetuosity are shown by the angle of the low-set thumbs (denoting ego yet again) which will frequently land her in hot water. Highset lines on the hand? That means she sets high goals for herself and always strives to reach them, even though sometimes she may feel she isn't good enough, for the Jupiter fingers which control self-esteem are short and low set. Perhaps her family background left her with some conflicting hang-ups? I sensed that she sometimes feels isolated, perhaps even unloved, and this would diminish her self-respect. However, as we've seen, Apollo and thumbs are healthily-placed so her ego can soon bump her back into a positive frame of mind.

·P·R·O·F·I·L·E·

Actress, star of the *Carry On* films

Date of Birth: 6 August 1937

Sun Sign: LEO

Element: Fire

Ruling Planet: Sun (Apollo)

BARBARA WINDSOR

Barbara's definitely a survivor: her hands are small, square and just slightly rounded, with tight skin, full of inner strength and staying power. So, oddly enough, the very tininess of her hands really shows how capable she is; as the compact

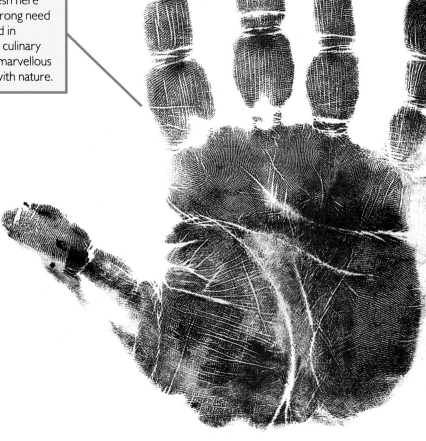

FINGERTIPS
All nicely balanced, lean and round – shows her appreciation of things spiritual: Barbara knows there is a purpose to our presence on this planet. Attests to a powerful mentality also.

APOLLO FINGER
Long and strong giving freedom of thought and action, healthy ego, artistic confidence, need for others' admiration and a love of people. Leans towards Saturn showing loneliness cannot be tolerated. This is the typical finger length of a Leo, proud and purposeful.

PHALANGES
Protruding flesh here relates to a strong need to be involved in domestic and culinary affairs, and a marvellous attunement with nature.

AT HOME IN HER HOME

Barbara would be an excellent hostess, cook, homemaker – if she had the time! For the base of the Jupiter and Saturn fingers are pronounced, denoting a love of cooking, and of course the home environment offers balance and warmth which would make her feel very secure, provided she was surrounded by friendly company.

AT HOME IN THE THEATRE?

It's odd but there are very few signs in the hand that point to any theatrical involvement, except for the small Mercury lines drawing attention to the powerful Mercury mount. Mercury encourages verbal or musical talents so its prominence gives some evidence of Barbara's creative abilities. The head line, particularly on the left hand, has a small fork at the end which implies a facility for writing. This, together with the Mercury finger, points to her desires – too deep to be ignored – to communicate, and her continuously active brain.

SERIOUS SEXINESS

We all know Barbara's public persona and her fleshy palms, robust and earthy, bear out her enjoyment of all life's frivolities and physical pleasures! They exude sexual charisma and body language. She would cherish her partner well if she trusted his commitment to her. In fact, when you add the liberally-shaped mounts Venus and Moon to the fleshy texture of the palm you can see that she'll make him feel he is the main priority in her life! But there is femininity alongside the lust: the thumbs are easy-going and low set. So Barbara is not only passionate, she is caring and sensitive as well.

SERIOUS SENSE

The squareness of the tip of the Saturn finger and its overall length compared with the rest of

the hand reveals a serious, thoughtful side. But this is a side she hides, for though she is self-contained I sensed some fear and inadequacy in her; her character is deeply, even painfully philosophical. Only those close to her would detect her apprehensions and gloom but of course the ego will help dispel any long-term depression. She's very open-minded (see the low-set thumbs and clearly-spaced lines), especially to spiritual ideas, and receptive to extra-sensory suggestion; the wide fingertips leave lots of room for way-out ideas. Further down, the fingers lie closer together, as do the companionship lines on mount Venus, meaning that she hates to be alone.

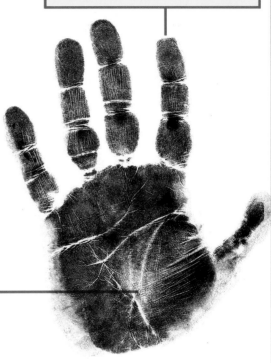

THE PAST HAND

JUPITER FINGER

The shortness dampens dreams and spirits but although its curve shows inventive scheming, it lacks the power to put ideas to good use. Planning may be left to others and relying on them puts Barbara in a vulnerable position. Low set also, reinforcing this inadequacy.

LIFE LINE

Left line broken showing a radical change in lifestyle age 45–48; since the life line's unbroken in the right hand it suggests Barbara has overcome the shock. But the wounds are not completely healed – the line on the left is just beginning to knit together. In another couple of years the line may be completely restored to normality. Compare the break on the head line that echoes this. Fate, however, is taking over strongly and putting her back on the right track.

Fate overshadows the life line and between her early 30s and 40s she lost lots of energy through stress and strain at home. Disturbances in this erratic period have really touched her deeply, making it difficult for her to shrug off the past. But although swamped by problems, she would have been forced by fate to seek outside interests to distract herself from personal setbacks. Work would have been a life saver! Her inner nature may have been bruised but she's gained strength along the way, so she can now face the dramas of life with renewed vigour. Like I said, a true survivor.

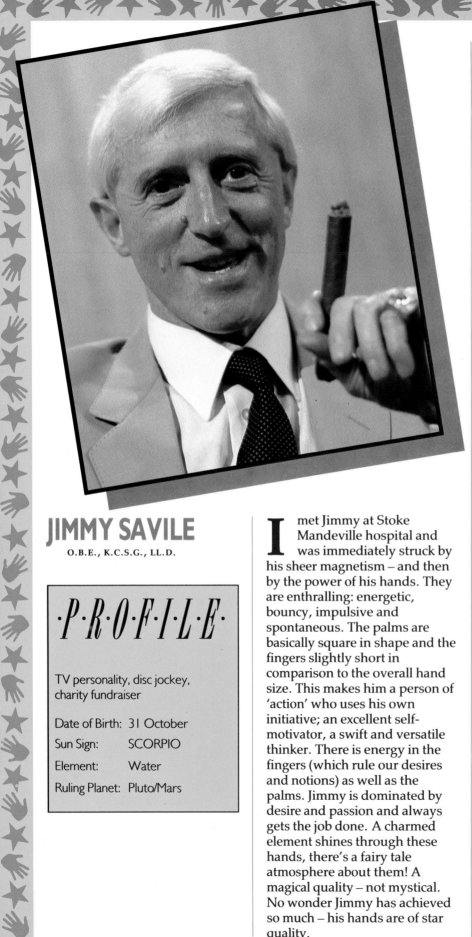

JIMMY SAVILE

O.B.E., K.C.S.G., LL.D.

·P·R·O·F·I·L·E·

TV personality, disc jockey, charity fundraiser

Date of Birth: 31 October

Sun Sign: SCORPIO

Element: Water

Ruling Planet: Pluto/Mars

I met Jimmy at Stoke Mandeville hospital and was immediately struck by his sheer magnetism – and then by the power of his hands. They are enthralling: energetic, bouncy, impulsive and spontaneous. The palms are basically square in shape and the fingers slightly short in comparison to the overall hand size. This makes him a person of 'action' who uses his own initiative; an excellent self-motivator, a swift and versatile thinker. There is energy in the fingers (which rule our desires and notions) as well as the palms. Jimmy is dominated by desire and passion and always gets the job done. A charmed element shines through these hands, there's a fairy tale atmosphere about them! A magical quality – not mystical. No wonder Jimmy has achieved so much – his hands are of star quality.

BEHIND THE SMILE

The private side of this man can be surprisingly uncertain, bottling up doubt and unpredictable thoughts. However, he can make up for this and overcome his insecurities positively. I don't think Jimmy allows too many negative issues to stand in his way for he has a bulldozer-like inner drive. He throws himself enthusiastically into life and living. I'm certain he has a good sense of direction and feels he is fulfilling some sort of true purpose.

A SHOWMAN AT HEART

There's a sensual overtone to these palms; Jimmy can display his affection in many ways, but not necessarily always through hugs, kisses or one-to-one unions. There is a gentler, more sensitive side to his nature and he can fulfil his desires and yearnings in other ways. I do think however that Jimmy does everything with a certain amount of loud showmanship. He likes to be seen and heard!

There's also a sort of clumsy sensation revealed in the physical part of the hand and I wonder if he tends to be over-forceful in this area of his life. In affairs of the heart he could well be a bit of a rascal, a ladies' man, and a little gullible where the passions are concerned. His sexual behaviour may come across as strong and lusty, allowing actions to rule when the mood is ripe. So – a person whose sexual attitude could be just too much for some!

STRIVING AND THRIVING...

The whole combination of lines, particularly those spreading across the inner part of both palms (from centre hand to Venus) shows that Jimmy very much likes to 'belong' to the world. He loves being adored and wanted, maybe as a substitute for something missing

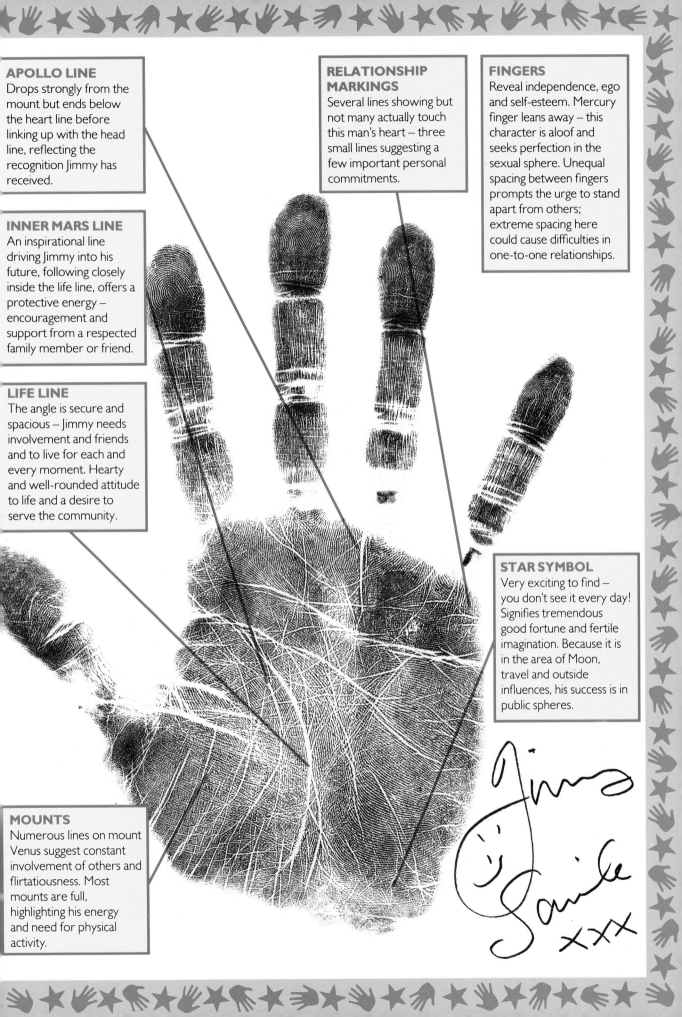

APOLLO LINE
Drops strongly from the mount but ends below the heart line before linking up with the head line, reflecting the recognition Jimmy has received.

INNER MARS LINE
An inspirational line driving Jimmy into his future, following closely inside the life line, offers a protective energy – encouragement and support from a respected family member or friend.

LIFE LINE
The angle is secure and spacious – Jimmy needs involvement and friends and to live for each and every moment. Hearty and well-rounded attitude to life and a desire to serve the community.

RELATIONSHIP MARKINGS
Several lines showing but not many actually touch this man's heart – three small lines suggesting a few important personal commitments.

FINGERS
Reveal independence, ego and self-esteem. Mercury finger leans away – this character is aloof and seeks perfection in the sexual sphere. Unequal spacing between fingers prompts the urge to stand apart from others; extreme spacing here could cause difficulties in one-to-one relationships.

STAR SYMBOL
Very exciting to find – you don't see it every day! Signifies tremendous good fortune and fertile imagination. Because it is in the area of Moon, travel and outside influences, his success is in public spheres.

MOUNTS
Numerous lines on mount Venus suggest constant involvement of others and flirtatiousness. Most mounts are full, highlighting his energy and need for physical activity.

in earlier life that left him needing recognition and admiration. But you can see some marvellously encouraging markings in this area of the palm, many small lines growing upward and outward from the life line showing success resulting from his own efforts. Dedication has paid off. Jimmy has a restless spirit and, although commitments are very important to him, basically he is a mover and a traveller. The greater the challenge the better; he thrives on risks and has no visible fear of attempting testing ventures. I found a balanced leaning towards physical, mental and spiritual energies: qualities that make for a happy and contented person if kept under control. He is boisterous, impetuous and mischievous, with a good sense of humour – albeit dry – and can remain slightly detached from the world.

HEAD IN THE CLOUDS?

Jimmy has a very fanciful imagination and can sometimes be too sensitive. Thanks to the active area of Neptune (and of course his ruling planet Pluto) we can see that the imagination is sometimes unsatisfied, making him irritable and vulnerable. These creative channels must be used all the time (it's here Jimmy applies most of his energies) looking for new ideas and challenging projects. The head line lies high on the palm showing that he is not solely fanciful, but it does get a bit erratic and detached at intervals, making him seek new departures. You can see the lines splitting on several occasions; that shows he can dramatically change his thought process whenever he chooses.

FATE AND THE FUTURE

Just glancing at the fate area of the right palm we see that Jimmy has not left much to destiny. He seems to have got to work on his life at a very early age, leaving little to circumstances, for the fate line is broken and scattered and starts late. Fate intervenes more in latter years which means that although Jimmy has had more freedom of choice of his personal affairs in the past he may find as maturity sets in destiny will also. But up to now he has had more control than most of us!

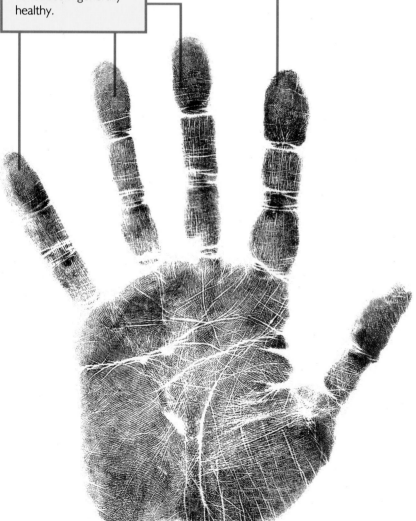

TIRED LINES
Found on the fingertips, these indicate the need for more rest, although hands seem generally healthy.

THE PAST HAND

Jimmy is a fighter and a survivor, no matter what debris he has to push through. He has a streak of impulsiveness and heaps of perseverance. There is an ounce or two of isolation and retreat but a whole pound of warmth and generosity. I must confess to standing in awe of these palms for they certainly have a magical element and a feeling of 'it was all meant to be'.

ROY KINNEAR

·P·R·O·F·I·L·E·

Actor and comedian

Date of Birth: 8 January 1934

Sun Sign: CAPRICORN

Element: Earth

Ruling Planet: Saturn

Puffy, full, round palms – everything that leans towards an active, involved, enthusiastic and physical man. The shape of the palm where it joins the base of the fingers slopes heavily from Jupiter down to Mercury, showing just how hard Roy has had to work for his living. These are sorrowful, struggling hands, but busy and kind with no regrets or wasted opportunities.

TRUE GRIT

Roy has enormous stamina in the Jupiter and Mars quarter of his palm, extending into Venus (thick joints and phalanges) so his inner drive and respect for life never flags. But having said that, Jupiter may be too dominant and encourage so much energy that Roy can't ever relax. And on top of this the prominence of the Mars areas (the planet of aggression and drive) gives him a propensity to rush into things and get totally engrossed. Spontaneity is seen in the short Jupiter finger, the pugnacity of Mars and the spirit of energy along the head lines. Mars may make him restless and frustrated sometimes, and his temper ragged. If his palms are always as red as they were when we met,

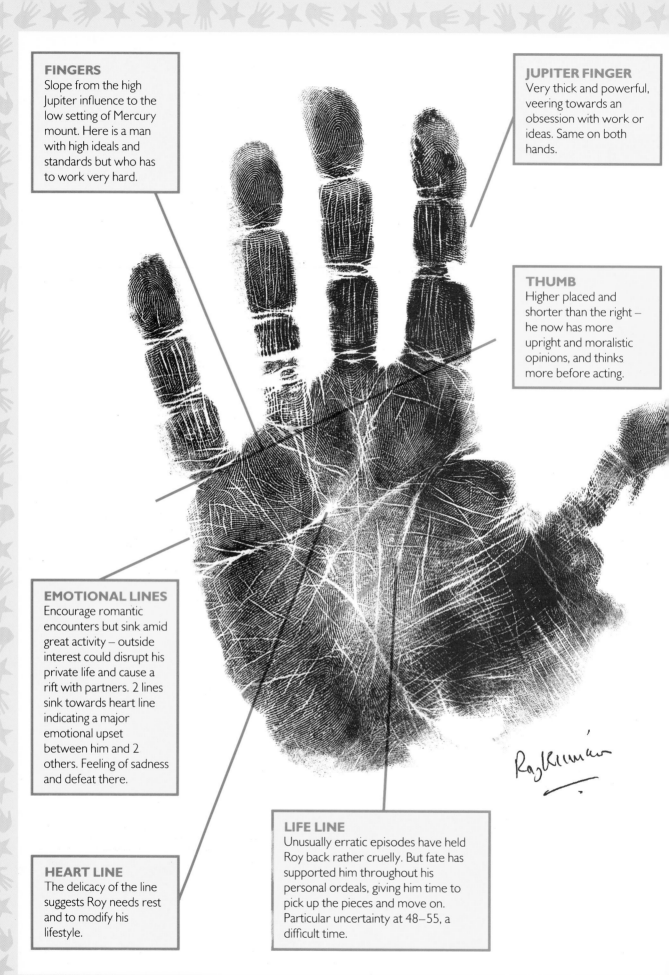

FINGERS
Slope from the high Jupiter influence to the low setting of Mercury mount. Here is a man with high ideals and standards but who has to work very hard.

JUPITER FINGER
Very thick and powerful, veering towards an obsession with work or ideas. Same on both hands.

THUMB
Higher placed and shorter than the right – he now has more upright and moralistic opinions, and thinks more before acting.

EMOTIONAL LINES
Encourage romantic encounters but sink amid great activity – outside interest could disrupt his private life and cause a rift with partners. 2 lines sink towards heart line indicating a major emotional upset between him and 2 others. Feeling of sadness and defeat there.

HEART LINE
The delicacy of the line suggests Roy needs rest and to modify his lifestyle.

LIFE LINE
Unusually erratic episodes have held Roy back rather cruelly. But fate has supported him throughout his personal ordeals, giving him time to pick up the pieces and move on. Particular uncertainty at 48–55, a difficult time.

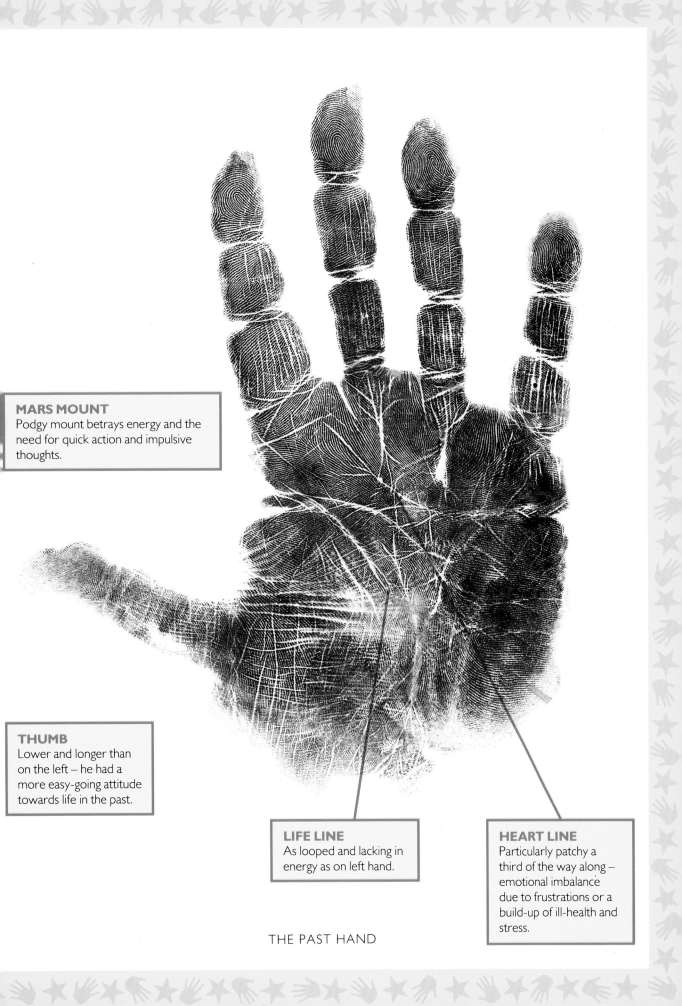

MARS MOUNT
Podgy mount betrays energy and the need for quick action and impulsive thoughts.

THUMB
Lower and longer than on the left – he had a more easy-going attitude towards life in the past.

LIFE LINE
As looped and lacking in energy as on left hand.

HEART LINE
Particularly patchy a third of the way along – emotional imbalance due to frustrations or a build-up of ill-health and stress.

THE PAST HAND

then they reinforce Mars' pent-up emotions. Roy couldn't tell me if this was the case but he certainly needs to relax in order to calm the excess of emotion in his system.

LIONHEART

Yet in these robust palms the heart line is positively endearing – a sweet mixture of sensitivity, strong emotions and tremendous giving. The line rises right up to Jupiter mount, giving him intensely high ideals, and a strange marking is creeping across Jupiter desperately trying to make contact with the heart line – there's a real sense of emotional striving and purpose here protecting Roy from the negative side of life. He has a questioning heart and passions can overtake him completely, but he's appealing and sensual rather than overtly sexual. He's a warm, friendly, home-loving bear who revels in the security of his attachment to others (see the large, airy mount Venus, deep heart lines and fleshy emotional areas of the upper palm). The powerful presence of Jupiter also drives his emotions making him respond passionately to any job in hand, with devotion and an earthy enthusiasm. There's some delicacy in the line that may relate to the organ itself, it's rather frayed a third of the way down, so Roy needed to watch his health in his late 40s, early 50s. You can see a similar sapping of energy in the life line at this time when some major pressure must have been at work.

So, delicacy within, but there's a tough outer shell to these palms, a strong, thick skin texture. Roy can protect himself and maintain an outer calm even while hurting or raging inside. This detachment is reinforced by the separation of the Mercury finger from Apollo, a breathing space which creates a barrier to keep intruders out.

FIRM FOUNDATION

Roy's life lines are erratic and make me think he ambles through life in a rather disorganised way. Their scattered effect show major upheavals that have cast him down, but the fate line always takes over, eager to retrieve the situation. As the fate line links up strongly from mount Venus we know that a solid family background has helped him weather the storms; the home base and upbringing have kept him on the straight and narrow path of morality, and always provide comfort, protection and retreat. An amazing number of lines cross mount Venus showing how overwhelmingly important human contact has been in his life.

AS TIME GOES BY

The palms bear witness to change as the years pass: Roy's right (past for Roy is left-handed) hand is narrower and less curved than the current hand, the thumb is lower placed and longer, but the fingers have hardly changed at all – his desires are still much the same – and the top of the palm still slopes down towards Mercury – he continues to give as much as he can to the job in hand. Overall his personality is less rebellious and he has more respect for rules and obligations (left hand more robust and rounded, life line active, head line longer). The intense sloping of the fingers doesn't just speak of hard work, it whispers of sadness and striving to improve. Mercury and fate lines blend, suggesting that speech and drama was the inevitable route for him to follow, a gift passed down through his family.

ROVING SPIRIT, ROVING EYE

Travel reigns in these palms: look at the outer edge of Moon, particularly on the left hand. This means Roy not only loves to travel abroad but also in the realms of his fertile imagination. He is a man of the world, enquiring and curious. Several romantic adventures are to be seen higher up the hand; the emotional lines show two or three serious attachments, but two slope down toward the heart line showing disappointment. Maybe outside influences got in the way? There are irrational markings interfering all over this area; any partner of Roy's would have to compete with his other self-indulgent interests. And if they can't, well his alternative outlets would always help to comfort him.

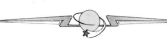

So here we have a man ruled by his physical passions but who unfortunately allows too many frustrations to build up. He should take time out to restore his equilibrium. A fine, vigorous spirit who's overcome many a hardship, a man of the world who cannot bear to be shut off from society. Genuine, sincere, kind, but overshadowed by some sadness that I can't pinpoint exactly. Although his ruling planet is Saturn that influence is wholly subordinate to the motivating strength of Jupiter and Mars.

SUSANNAH YORK

·P·R·O·F·I·L·E·

Actress

Date of Birth: 9 January

Sun Sign: CAPRICORN

Element: Earth

Ruling Planet: Saturn

Susannah is the owner of powerfully proud and purposeful hands. She has heavy masculine palms but elegant extended feminine fingers. The palms with their broad thick base are driven forward by Earth's influence; all natural elements would be highly respected, and everything to do with the conservation of the planet is relevant to Susannah. The left palm is larger in size, governing the nature with its full gentle arching; this reveals inherent artistic talents, encouraging all pursuits in the outside environment. Susannah has great expectations – her ideas are sometimes out of reach! She expects extremely high standards from others and certainly expects the best returns from her own efforts.

FAST FORWARD

Note how Mercury stands adamantly apart from its slimmer brother Apollo rejecting Apollo's warmth from time to time. This shows an ability to act on her own initiative (she houses many a wilful notion), and gives a feeling of pushing others away, a need for total uniqueness. This need to be free unto her own laws is passionately essential to Susannah. It shows in the broad sweeping lines, as does an intense dislike of restricting circumstances or long-term commercial obligations. The generous thumbs, and tall Apollo fingers with their rounded tips indicate warmth of character and a cheerful and fun-loving disposition, but the sombre Saturn rules (see the rather overbearing Saturn digit), making for a serious nature. So it's work first for Susannah, play and leisure second. Everything in these palms is forward moving, no grudges are held. She has an inbuilt natural ability to conquer and thrive.

GOD GIVEN GRACE

Graceful must be the correct description for such a sensuous, romantic person. Susannah shows a delicate girdle of Venus, its scattered nature confirming her hypersensitivity and tendency to be easily offended over small matters. The girdle links with the heart line, revealing impulses and instincts which can lead her into deep waters. There is an abundance of giving in these palms – the many, many lines crossing at Mercury mount along with the liberal thumbs and tender Jupitarian heart lines reveal a person capable of great penetrating love, but sadly, lack of communication between Mercury/Apollo fingers will not always allow her true emotions to show. Although she is not averse to new experiments, particularly in the sexual sphere, and may go to great lengths to achieve satisfaction, the heart line at one stage was quite straight and rigid, holding the emotions in check (see the horizontal line between the lower Mercury and Apollo mounts). Most probably the circumstances must be just right before Susannah's deepest feelings can be expressed.

FORCEFUL AND FIERY

The head and life lines start high on mount Jupiter giving a great air of personal authority to the palms and reflecting Susannah's fastidiousness and high standards. The head line slopes deeply, emphasising inbuilt logic, strength of purpose plus ambition – managing people should be a piece of cake. However, there is a rather impetuous and impatient look to the head line (see the flurry of intruding markings, middle line, and how on the right hand it breaks at the end revealing a quick temper). I found Susannah's hands less flexible than anticipated, showing she has great authority over her own feelings and can master situations with some shrewdness. The thumbs are both very long and we can assume her ancestors were highly intellectual. The lower phalanges are slightly narrow revealing a certain gullibility – she gives into temptations occasionally – but for the most part, the will power (top phalange) dominates.

TIRED LINES
Markings of tiredness that result from a heavy workload. She needs to pace her energies and routines. Meditation would be invaluable for such a hyperactive brain and restless body.

TALENT/EMPATHY LINES
These are far too numerous for Susannah's life ever to be dull! There's constant drama and involvement for her which, because of the abundance of markings, unfortunately overshadows personal spheres and relationships.

HEART LINE
Though long and loving, running up to Jupiter, the line is straight and restricted at this point holding back her emotions sometimes.

FOUR FATE LINES
It's astonishing to find so many! One and two run from the Moon mount indicating outside influences and a career in the public sector. Three runs from the base of the hand up to the head line exaggerating the power of her mind and talent with her voice. Four runs from Venus indicating a solid home background, and links with the head line denoting intelligence and creativity yet again.

DOUBLE LIFE LINE
Clear example of a close spiritual connection in Susannah's life that is enormously supportive.

INCENTIVE LINE
Marvellous marking running off the fourth fate line up towards Apollo. Could show enormous professional recognition mid-life.

1   2   3   4

Susannah Mark

THE PAST HAND

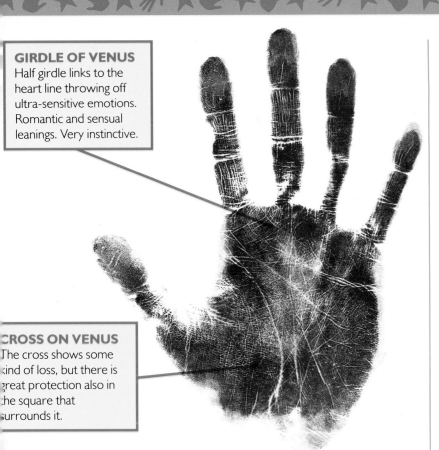

GIRDLE OF VENUS
Half girdle links to the heart line throwing off ultra-sensitive emotions. Romantic and sensual leanings. Very instinctive.

CROSS ON VENUS
The cross shows some kind of loss, but there is great protection also in the square that surrounds it.

FOURFOLD FATE

Extraordinary! Susannah has four fate lines! The first, running so strongly and far out over the Moon mount, suggests she was born abroad or that 'distance' or unusual circumstances somehow surrounded her birth. The second line runs over Moon linking with the head line. Because of its outside connection it's easy to see why Susannah has achieved so much success via her art and contact with the public, especially as part of it branches off towards Apollo (the area of fulfilment in career, people and the arts). It seems fame was deemed from birth – surely this lady must always have been aware of a burning sense of purpose. The third fate line gathers its energies from the base of the palm running up to the head line, and reveals a wonderfully exciting imagination, creative powers of speech and sound intelligence. Another pointer to her artistic prosperity! Susannah is blessed with an extraordinary nature and a certain spiritual awareness. A strong spiritual link is projected in the fourth fate line joining head to life line, from the area of Venus. This offers Susannah an unseen protector whom I intuitively felt had been linked to the theatre when on this earth plane. The inspiration emanating from this 'guide' envelops Susannah so strongly that the impression remained with me long after I left her home. Confirmation of this helpful and protective 'guide' is revealed through the double life line, but its presence suggests that she may well need that protection more than most. The linking of the third and fourth fate lines to the head line emphasises an inventive, intellectual mind with the ability to write creatively or to draw, offering her further interests outside the theatre. The fourth, stemming from Venus denotes a firm background from childhood, but one which I felt may have been severely regimented at times. Perhaps a military father or parents with Victorian views?

DOMESTIC DRAMAS

At the base of the thumb where it links with Venus we see a loop and several crosses showing Susannah's private life has certainly had its fair share of sudden crises and decisions. I felt that the emotions were rather widespread in this region of the palm; it is possible that full emotional satisfaction is yet to be experienced. A cross on the Venus mount (right hand) around her late forties reveals a termination/relinquishment? Possibly of a relationship or an old lifestyle? A drama which Susannah may overreact to, for the ultra-sensitive markings centre of the palm confirm she often sees the worst in a situation.

There's an almost 'little girl lost' image in these charming but forceful palms. An unspoilt quality of purity and grandeur – a grace unusual in our age, which is retained forever. She can seem clumsy in her mannerisms – out of synch at times with our modern world; but her impressionable personality and dedicated intellectual mind move her onwards aiming to exploit the best from life. Her inner timing and methodical attitudes are unsurpassable. I'm certain there are some favourable professional rewards ahead in her late forties and age 51. Friends travel with her through life, faithful companions (see the abundant markings on mounts Venus and Mercury) whom she will value as she values all things. Her temper may flash out sometimes yet she can control it, dampening the flame of passion quickly – but not completely. For there is a true burning in these hands, a yearning deep down for 'something' that defies exact analysis. Susannah prepares herself for the worst and accepts the best!

NICHOLAS LYNDHURST

·P·R·O·F·I·L·E·

Actor, star of *Only Fools and Horses* and *The Two of Us*

Date of Birth: 20 April 1961

Sun Sign: ARIES

Element: Fire

Ruling Planet: Mars

Nick's a dreamer, betrayed by the extreme elasticity of his hands. He's impressionable, swayed by outside opinions and people and by however he happens to feel at the moment. He's probably quite happy to let others make the decisions. What he needs is a comfortable backdrop to his laid-back life where he can indulge his intellectual fascination for the arts and beauty, colours and shapes. This is all emphasised by his long sensuous fingers and the almost poetic slope of the hand. There are psychic and idealistic leanings which spark off his curiosity. Despite being a dreamer he'll always work everything out in his mind in intense detail – but there may not be much logic involved! His skin is dainty and fine – practically too soft to touch – so I'm sure that he's very responsive to climatic conditions.

Nick doesn't have an overly strong constitution; patchy skin and faint lines reveal that he needs to eat carefully and watch his sleep or vital energy will run out too quickly. He's probably irritatingly prone to catching viruses, colds and coughs, so I think he should cosset himself a bit, especially in the winter or when working under great pressure.

TALENT GALORE
Nick's Apollo finger is very long and the mount covered with lines, reflecting a love of music, drama and theatre: he derives great pleasure from the finer things in life. Mercury mount is similarly well lined, bursting with communication skills, so he's undoubtedly picked the right métier. He can inject all these powers of expression into his acting plus the extrovertness you can also detect. Further talent lines run over Apollo and Mercury mount giving him other avenues to explore when he wants a change!

TUNED IN
Psychic/idealistic shaped hands like these reveal penetrating insight, quick judgement and sound instincts but also a certain defencelessness. Nick's so in tune with life that he can act on impulse much more quickly than most of us. His attunement to life is underlined by the transparentness of his hands, suggesting uncluttered feelings.

AN INDEPENDENT IDEALIST
Wide spacing between fingers and head and heart lines equals a man studiously avoiding ongoing commitments! But beneath the carefree surface lies a warm and responsive nature who loves others – look how the long, graceful heart line rises to Jupiter. Comradeship is important but that doesn't mean he's at all ready to settle down and burden his independent life with responsibilities.

Nick's long, expansive fingers reveal his high ideals, his sturdy ambitions, his open-mindedness, inventiveness and tolerance. He'll always have a go at fulfilling his dreams no matter how way-out or out of reach they seem. But he should be careful not to lose his grip on reality altogether.

Fate seems to have had little influence on Nick; he usually directs himself or, more accurately, he allows someone else do so, as hinted by the active lines on the Moon and Venus mounts. The Moon mount is so busy that it's likely his fate lies outside the home base, and as the Moon is a creative influence this links with his theatrical vocation. But however he fulfils his dreams, he's led and loved by so many others around him that he'll never be lonely.

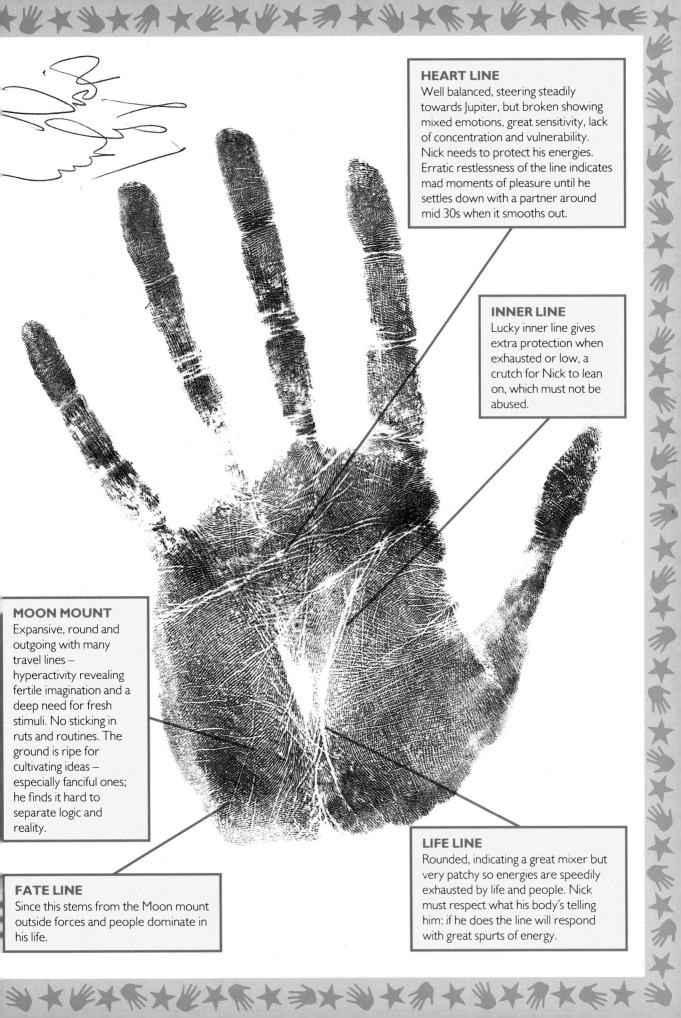

HEART LINE
Well balanced, steering steadily towards Jupiter, but broken showing mixed emotions, great sensitivity, lack of concentration and vulnerability. Nick needs to protect his energies. Erratic restlessness of the line indicates mad moments of pleasure until he settles down with a partner around mid 30s when it smooths out.

INNER LINE
Lucky inner line gives extra protection when exhausted or low, a crutch for Nick to lean on, which must not be abused.

MOON MOUNT
Expansive, round and outgoing with many travel lines – hyperactivity revealing fertile imagination and a deep need for fresh stimuli. No sticking in ruts and routines. The ground is ripe for cultivating ideas – especially fanciful ones; he finds it hard to separate logic and reality.

FATE LINE
Since this stems from the Moon mount outside forces and people dominate in his life.

LIFE LINE
Rounded, indicating a great mixer but very patchy so energies are speedily exhausted by life and people. Nick must respect what his body's telling him: if he does the line will respond with great spurts of energy.

SUE ARMSTRONG

·P·R·O·F·I·L·E·

Author of *Star Palms*

Date of Birth: 26 August, 1947

Sun Sign: VIRGO

Element: Earth

Ruling Planet: Mercury

Sue has been a spiritual counsellor and palm reader for seven years and has been collecting the palm prints for this book for the past 18 months. An avid fan of theatre and film, she lives near the sea in Sussex with her husband and daughter.

Since childhood she has been aware of an inner spiritual force which is evident to her through dreams, premonitions and meditation. It has been her guide through life's trials and tribulations, and she tries to live her life according to its promptings.

ACKNOWLEDGEMENTS

The following photographs are copyright: Stephanie Beacham, James Globus/Rex Features Ltd (cover), Rex Features; Barry Humphries, Universal Pictorial Press and Agency Ltd; Michael Aspel, LWT; Cynthia Payne, Rex Features Ltd; Sue Cook, BBC; Gloria Hunniford, Tim Roney/*Radio Times* (cover), LWT; Derek Jameson, Monitor Syndication; Fred Dinenage, TVS Television Ltd; Beryl Reid, Monitor Syndication; Derek Griffiths, Stollmar Productions; Dorothy Tutin, Universal Pictorial Press and Agency Ltd; June Brown, BBC Enterprises Ltd; Matthew Kelly, 'Ouandaries' TVS Television Ltd; Barbara Windsor, Rex Features Ltd; Jimmy Savile, Rex Features Ltd; Roy Kinnear, Rex Features Ltd, Universal Pictorial Press and Agency Ltd; Susannah York, Peter Brooker/Rex Features Ltd; Nicholas Lyndhurst, Nils Jorgensen/Rex Features Ltd.